Pollution and Freshwater Fish

Pollution and Freshwater Fish

Richard Lloyd

OBE, BSc, FIBiol, FIFM, FZS
Formerly of the *Fisheries Laboratory*, Burnham-on-Crouch
Ministry of Agriculture, Fisheries and Food, UK

A Buckland Foundation Book

Fishing News Books

DISTRIBUTORS

Marston Book Services Ltd
PO Box 87
Oxford OX2 0DT
(*Orders*: Tel: 0865 240201
         Fax: 0865 721205
         Telex: 83355 MEDBOK G)

USA
Blackwell Scientific Publications Inc.
3 Cambridge Center
Cambridge, MA 02142
(*Orders*: Tel: 800 759−6102
           617 225−0401)

Canada
Oxford University Press
70 Wynford Drive
Don Mills
Ontario M3C 1J9
(*Orders*: Tel: 416 441−2941)

Australia
Blackwell Scientific Publications
(Australia) Pty Ltd
54 University Street
Carlton, Victoria 3053
(*Orders*: Tel: 03 347−0300)

British Library
Cataloguing in Publication Data

Lloyd, Richard
  Pollution and freshwater fish.
  I. Title
  597.05222

  ISBN 0−85238−187−5

A Pioneer of Fishery Research

Frank Buckland 1826–1880

THE MAN AND HIS WORK

Frank Buckland was an immensely popular mid-Victorian writer and lecturer on natural history, a distinguished public servant and a pioneer in the study of the problems of the commercial fisheries. He was born in 1826, the first child of William Buckland DD FRS, the first Professor of Geology in Oxford who was an eminent biologist himself. From infancy Frank was encouraged to study the world about him and he was accustomed to meeting the famous scientists who visited his father. Like many other biologists of his day, he trained as a surgeon; in 1854 he was gazetted Assistant Surgeon to the Second Life Guards, having completed his training at St George's Hospital, London. He began to write popular articles on natural history and these were issued in book form in 1857 as 'Curiosities of Natural History'. It was an immediate success and was to be followed at intervals by three more volumes; although long out of print these can be found in second-hand bookshops and still provide entertainment and interest.

His success increased demands upon him as a writer and lecturer and he resigned his Commission in 1863. He had become interested in fish culture, then regarded simply as the rearing of fish from the egg. This involved the fertilization of eggs stripped by hand from ripe fish with milt similarly obtained. Release of fry was seen as a means of improving fisheries, particularly of salmon and trout, in rivers and lakes which had suffered from over-exploitation or pollution. He gave a successful lecture on the subject at the Royal Institution in 1863, subsequently published as 'Fish Hatching', and was struck by the intense interest aroused by his demonstration.

He was permitted to set up a small fish hatchery at the South Kensington Museum, the forerunner of the Science Museum, and by 1865 had collected there a range of exhibits which were to form the nucleus of his Museum of Economic Fish Culture. This aimed to inform the public about the fish and fisheries of the British Isles and for the rest of his life he laboured to develop this display. Although he was paid for his attendances at the Museum, the exhibits were provided by him at his own expense; in his will he gave the Collection to the nation.

National concern over many years at the decline of salmon fisheries, which suffered not only from overfishing and pollution but also extensive poaching and obstructions such as locks and weirs, led in 1861 to the passing of the Salmon Fisheries Act under which two Inspectors for England and Wales were appointed. When one of the original Inspectors resigned in 1867, Buckland was an obvious choice as successor. He had already accompanied the Inspectors on their visits to rivers and was also often asked for advice by riparian owners. He would think nothing of plunging into a river in winter to help net fish for the collection of eggs, a practice which probably led to his early death. Until 1866 he produced a steady stream of natural history articles mainly for 'The Field'. Then he helped to establish a rival journal, Land and Water, which he supported until his death.

Britain's growing population in the last century created many problems of food supply; the sea fisheries offered a cheap source of abundant first class protein and as a result the marine fisheries, and particularly the North Sea fisheries, grew spectacularly. Little was known about sea fish; no statistics of fish landings were available, at least in England, and the biological basis of fisheries was a mystery, though it was widely believed that marine fisheries were inexhaustible. Nevertheless there were disturbing indications that previously prolific fisheries were no longer profitable and many Royal Commissions were set up. The most famous was that of 1863, which had Thomas Henry Huxley as one of its members. Buckland himself sat on four Commissions between 1875 and his death, a fact which reflected his increasing standing as a fisheries expert.

During his lifetime a number of public fisheries exhibitions were held abroad, and he tirelessly pressed for something similar to be staged in the United Kingdom. Unfortunately he died before he could see his wish fulfilled, but there is no doubt that the exhibitions held in Norwich (1881), Edinburgh (1882) and London (1883) owed much to the public interest he had worked so hard to engender. It should be noted that the Marine Biological Association of the UK, with its famous laboratory at Plymouth, was a direct result of the enthusiasm and concern created by the Great International Fisheries Exhibition held in London in 1883.

He died in December 1880, possibly of a disease caught from his parrot, for he had always been careless about his health and must have worked for long periods at full stretch to maintain such a high output of material. What he wrote was sometimes uneven but he was often breaking new ground. At all times he was concerned to explain, to teach and, most particularly to make the general public aware of the importance of their fisheries and the need to protect and develop this great national asset. A few days before his death he signed his will. His wife was to have a life interest in his estate but he bequeathed a sum of money which on her death should be used to establish a trust fund to support 'a professorship of Economic Fish Culture, to be called The Buckland Professorship'. The main responsibility laid on The Buckland Professor was that lectures should be delivered each year at suitable venues in the United Kingdom.

THE FOUNDATION

It is clear that Frank Buckland intended the term Fish Culture to be widely interpreted and to cover much more than fish hatching and the rearing of fry. Consequently, when the original £5000 endowment became available in 1926, after the death of his widow in 1921, the original Trustees of the Buckland Foundation took a broad view of the subjects that Buckland Professors should be invited to write and lecture about. In 1930, for example, the first Buckland lectures were given by Professor Garstang, a leading marine biologist of the time, on the subject of 'Frank Buckland's Life and Work'. The following year it was 'Salmon Hatching and Salmon Migrations' and after that 'The natural history of the herring in Scottish Waters'. As fisheries science and fishing methods evolved many subjects presented themselves which were unknown to Buckland and his contemporaries and succeeding Trustees have sought to ensure that such topics are covered so that the lectures have always been timely, important and of value and interest to those who depend for their livelihood on some aspect of fish and fishing. Each of the three Trustees holds office for a five-year period and the day-to-day business of the Foundation is managed by its Clerk.

In the Spring of each year there is a meeting of the Trustees at which the subject and the Buckland Professor for the following year is chosen. In accepting the invitation to hold office the nominee also accepts the responsibility for producing a text and giving at least three lectures at venues that provide the closest possible link with that area of fish and fishing being examined. The text has to be approved by the Trustees before the lectures are delivered. The Professor receives £700 for the delivery of the manuscript and £100, with expenses, for each lecture and a commemorative medal at the end of his year of office. More often than not the texts of the 43 Buckland Professors holding office so far have been published as books and copies of the more recent ones are available from Fishing News Books.

The Trustees feel that by continuing to keep alive, via the means willed to them through Frank Buckland's own inspiration, the memory of a man who dedicated his life to the improvement of the commercial fisheries of the British Isles they are helping, in their turn, to improve conditions in the present commercial fisheries. As the 50th Lecture in the series begins to come into view, they are hoping for increasing recognition of both Buckland, the Man and for the Foundation he instituted.

Contents

Preface

When I was invited to be the Buckland Professor for 1990—91, I had to select the topic for my three lectures. I noted that Mr H.D. Turing had chosen the subject of freshwater pollution when he held the Professorship in 1950, which by coincidence was the year that I began my research career in the Scientific Civil Service, initially with the former Water Pollution Research Laboratory (now incorporated into the Water Research Centre) and latterly with the Ministry of Agriculture, Fisheries and Food.

During the following forty years there has been a rapid expansion in research into the effects of pollution on aquatic life in general and fish in particular, in which I have played a part. At the same time, there has been a growing awareness by the general public of environmental issues and an appreciation of the need for clean waters. However, while it is true that discharges of chemicals from a variety of sources have damaged fisheries, there has been a tendency to exaggerate the magnitude of the effects and also to ascribe all detrimental effects to pollution. This tendency will persist so long as such events are newsworthy. There is a real need, therefore, for a wider appreciation of the scientific background to pollution and freshwater fisheries which can then lead to a more balanced assessment of the problem. In the past, government scientists have been slow to respond to this need.

The main purpose of this book is to introduce the technical non-specialist to the complexities of the subject through a balanced overall view. References are made to other publications that contain more advanced information on specific topics, and which provide an introduction to the considerable literature on them.

For the record, I would like to thank the Secretaries of the Scottish, Welsh and Yorkshire Branches of the Institute of Fisheries Management who made the arrangements for the three public lectures given under the auspices of the Buckland Foundation.

Finally, I must express my gratitude to the countless number of scientists throughout the world who have given me their advice and support during my career. I have been fortunate in being surrounded by helpful colleagues wherever I have worked. If this book fulfils its intended function, then the credit is due as much to them as to me.

1 Introduction

Our inland waters have a particular fascination for us. The expanses of lake waters surrounded by hills, and the unique habitat of the corridors through which the streams and rivers flow towards the sea, evoke a sense of timelessness and feelings of contentment. But the aquatic environment is showing signs – many of them unwelcome – of man's activities. And our freshwater fisheries have not escaped the effects of the main problem – the discharge of chemicals and wastes. This book describes post-war efforts to protect the fisheries from such pollution, and discusses the different approaches which have been made towards their preservation and restoration.

Before beginning to discuss these matters, this introduction begins with a brief overview of the water cycle and the effect of man's management, and mismanagement, on this resource.

THE WATER CYCLE

About 75% of the Earth's surface is covered by water. Most of this water, around 97.3%, is salty and is contained in the oceans. Water evaporates from the sea surface to gather as clouds in the atmosphere, and from here it precipitates as rain to the Earth's surface. Over 75% of the freshwater in the world is stored in the polar ice and glaciers and a further 23% is in groundwater below the surface of the Earth. Only a very small percentage is found in rivers and lakes.

Some of the rain which falls on our countryside is lost to the atmosphere by evaporation from the surface and by transpiration from plants. The remainder percolates through the

1

soil and is collected into streams, lakes and rivers and returned to the sea. The chemical composition of this water reflects the geology of the land from which it drains; if the underlying bedrock is granite, then the water will be 'soft', poor in calcium and slightly acid. On the other hand, water which comes from land overlying chalk will be 'hard', rich in calcium and slightly alkaline. Because the vegetation of granite upland areas is sparse, the drainage water will be poor in nutrients and contain very few plants. In contrast, the lowland chalk streams are highly productive with abundant weed growth. In between these two extremes are numerous other types of catchment area, producing water with different chemical characteristics.

These chemical properties of the water, together with the temperature and the speed of the water current, control the types and species of animals and plants which can live in different freshwater areas. Some organisms are adapted to fast-flowing streams whereas others thrive in sluggish rivers and lakes. So even in the absence of man's activities, our surface waters would support a rich and varied diversity of plant and animal communities depending on the type of terrain which they drain.

WATER MANAGEMENT

Although lakes and rivers contain only a very small proportion of the Earth's freshwater − 0.33 and 0.004% respectively − they have played an important part in the development of our civilization. They provided a necessary supply of drinking water, so that settlements developed along their banks. They provided a defensive barrier against attack, and a means of transport and communication between communities. The fish were harvested for food. Later, weirs were installed at intervals along the length of rivers and mills built to harness water power for grinding corn. These changed the general pattern of water velocities as well as forming barriers to the passage of migrating fish − barriers which were used to trap and

harvest the migrating salmon and eels. As the human population increased, so the landscape was changed. Forests were
cleared and crops planted, land was drained and tilled. Rivers
were canalized and watercourses straightened for flood prevention. Marshland was reclaimed and extensive drainage
systems built. Increasing amounts of water were abstracted
for public supply, industry and land irrigation. All these
activities have caused radical changes in the physical nature
of our rivers and lakes.

THE ONSET OF POLLUTION

Probably, very few of our watercourses are now in a 'natural'
state in terms of their configuration, average water velocity
and seasonal variations of flow rate. In densely populated
countries, most rivers have been changed to such an extent
that so long as the populations remain at their present levels,
our surface waters will not return to their primeval state.

In developed countries, the Industrial Revolution and the
growth of large conurbations led to significant changes in
river water chemistry. Heavy industries were developed which
abstracted and used large quantities of water and returned it
as effluents loaded with chemical residues. Mining of ores
and coal produced contaminated drainage waters and leachates
from slag heaps. The development of water-borne sewage
systems to replace earth closets led to great improvements in
public health, but the discharge of even the treated effluents
caused far-reaching changes to the quality of surface waters.
The animal and plant communities in these receiving waters
were drastically changed and in some areas they disappeared
completely. To some extent, all these changes were generally
regarded as an acceptable consequence of increased prosperity
and better standards of hygiene. This is a problem that now
faces the less developed countries.

Public concern about the deterioration of the water quality
of our rivers began to be voiced in the mid-19th century and
in the United Kingdom a series of Royal Commissions was

appointed to assess the situation and to make recommendations which could be translated into legislation. In his
book *River Pollution*, published in the Buckland Lecture series,
Turing (1952) provided a vivid description of this 100-year
period of river pollution, and Pentelow (1953) supplemented
this with a review of the then current treatment processes
and legislation.

It may seem strange that a century of such earnest endeavour
to protect the quality of our surface waters produced so little
in the way of apparent beneficial results. But as Turing (1952)
pointed out, a river was considered by the general public,
even in 1950, to be polluted only if it was a public nuisance,
that is, if the water was unfit to drink or offended the senses
of sight or smell. The presence or absence of fish was not
generally held to be important, even though there was specific
legislation to protect these species. Most people had little
leisure time to enjoy the countryside; work was all-important
and the saying, 'Where there's muck, there's brass' [i.e.
money]', probably sums up the public acceptance of a polluted
environment during those years. Food on the table was more
important than the preservation of the environment and this
understandable attitude can be found in the less developed
countries today as they strive for economic growth. So the
rivers draining the industrialized areas were allowed to remain
in a degraded condition.

However, by the mid-1950s, the tide of public opinion was
beginning to change. Increased prosperity, more leisure time,
and easier access to the countryside had led to a greater
awareness by the public of the environment around them. A
greater demand for domestic supplies of water also increased
the need for cleaner water.

As mentioned earlier, this book describes one aspect of this
renaissance − the restoration and protection of freshwater
fisheries. It is a personal view, based on experience gained
and research carried out during the past 40 years. It provides
an introduction to the countless scientific papers and publications which have been written on this subject.

SOURCES OF POLLUTION

It is necessary to consider in greater detail the various routes whereby chemicals can get into surface waters. These routes can be broadly divided into point sources and diffuse sources.

Point sources

When thinking about polluted waters, many people probably have a mental image of the end of a large pipe from which a foul dark liquid is spewed into an otherwise attractive river. Such situations were not uncommon in the past, and various Royal Commission reports in the late 19th century contain graphic accounts of their occurrence. Gas works were particular offenders, discharging large quantities of phenols and ammonia derived from the coke ovens in which the coal gas was produced. Later, the effluents from sewage treatment works became a problem when the practice of irrigating fields with sewage (on what were known as sewage farms) gave way to the use of the now familiar trickling filters and activated sludge plant. These effluents then entered the receiving water at a fixed point and became slowly diluted downstream.

After the early 1950s it became the policy to divert industrial effluents to sewage treatment works where they would become diluted with sewage and also benefit from the treatment provided. This was successful because some wastes were so strong that they could not be treated by bacterial oxidation unless they were first diluted and the bacteria provided with some form of additional nutrients.

However, this practice created new problems. In heavily industrialized areas, a large proportion of the sewage could be derived from industry. This could affect the efficiency of the sewage treatment processes, leading to a poor quality effluent which contained substantial quantities of the wastes derived from the industries connected to the sewerage system. The obvious solution was to pre-treat the wastes before discharge to the sewer, but in many of the old industrial centres there were small factories which did not have the space to install the necessary treatment plant. Thus the situation changed from one where many small industries were discharging wastes from numerous outlets into streams and rivers, to one where a single highly complex effluent was discharged at a single point. These and other sources of inputs of wastes into freshwaters are shown in Fig. 1.1.

This situation can be made more complex in those areas where the sewers receive rain water run-off from buildings, roads and paved areas. At times of heavy rainfall, the sewers can discharge directly to watercourses via storm-water overflows and so bypass the treatment works. Obviously, this storm sewage is diluted by the rainfall, but the initial discharge may contain scoured deposits from the sewer and so be strongly polluting. Although the flow in the receiving water-

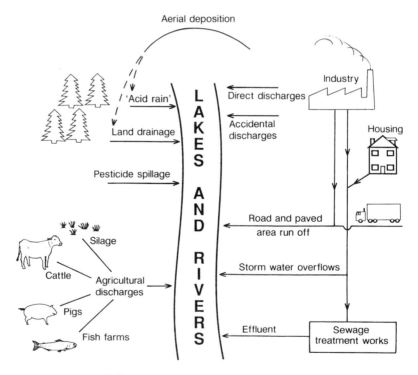

Fig. 1.1 Sources of chemical inputs into freshwater.

course will also increase with the rain run-off from the catchment area, this may occur some time after the initial discharge from the storm-water outfalls which might then initially receive only a minimal extra dilution in the receiving water.

Those sewage treatment works receiving mainly domestic sewage are not free from problems. An increase in the number of houses connected to the sewers, and a greater volume of water used for dishwashers and automatic washing machines can cause a hydraulic and organic overloading of the works. Expansion of the treatment facilities, especially in those areas where there has been considerable local urban development, may be prevented by the lack of suitable land space.

In one sense, these discharges from a multitude of domestic properties to the sewer can be considered as diffuse sources in the context of effluent control, even though their ultimate entry into the watercourse is at a single point. For example, the discharge of detergents from every household can only be primarily controlled by restricting the type of product used, rather than placing limits on the concentrations in the sewage effluent. In the early 1950s, the marketing of the new synthetic detergents as a substitute for soap powder caused considerable foaming at the sewage treatment works and at weirs on rivers. These detergents were resistant to biological breakdown and the problem was solved by the development and marketing of products that were rapidly degraded by the sewage treatment process.

All these potential or actual sources of pollution are obvious and so are well known, as are the direct discharges from rural industries, such as those making milk products, which may have their own treatment plants because the local sewage disposal works is too small or too far away to take the flow. But less obvious are the discharges from intensive agricultural practices, in particular the slurry from cattle sheds and drainage from silage production which are many times more polluting than untreated sewage. These wastes can enter watercourses as a result of flushing by heavy rain or by the breakdown of retaining walls built to contain the liquid.

Diffuse sources

The inputs described above are all from point sources, that is,
they are discharged into the watercourse via a pipe or from a
readily located installation. They claim the attention of the
public because they are often visible; they are readily ap-
preciable examples of something dirty being discharged into
something clean. This is in marked contrast to the other main
group of inputs, which is from diffuse sources, coming either
from the atmosphere or land.

Atmospheric
Perhaps the best known example of an atmospheric input is
that of acid rain, caused in part by the discharge to the
atmosphere of sulphur and nitrogen oxides from the burning
of fossil fuels, and in part from the spreading of animal
manures on land. But falling rain can also absorb other
chemicals in the atmosphere that are either present because
they are volatile (such as some pesticides) or because they are
present in small particles or dust (such as some metals). The
concentrations of such substances are very low, but in some
cases the contribution of the direct input to water from land
can be significant. Although these inputs are dependent on
rainfall and are therefore intermittent, the source is always
present. In the same way, a change in the vegetation of the
catchment area can alter the chemical characteristics of the
drainage water; for example, the planting of conifers on
moorland can increase the acidity of the local streams, and
part of this increase may be due to atmospheric contamination
being trapped by the foliage.

Terrestrial
The most obvious potential cause of pollution from a land
source is from the use of pesticides, especially insecticides
and herbicides, because the spraying operations are a common sight in the countryside. These chemicals can enter the
watercourse either in the dissolved state or attached to soil
particles in the land run-off water. Herbicides can, with special

permission, be used to control waterweeds and in some countries insecticides are used against the aquatic stages of insects such as mosquitos which carry disease. Another recently recognized source of pesticides in water is from the use of anti-fouling paints on pleasure craft; the biocide which kills the organisms that settle on the hull can leach into the surrounding water and harm sensitive species some distance away. These can all be regarded as diffuse inputs.

To conclude this series of examples of different sources of chemical input, there are the accidental discharges arising from road accidents, from bankside industry (such as wood preservatives from timber treatment), and the careless disposal of surplus pesticides.

Variability of inputs

The descriptions given above do not amount to a list of all the possible types of input but they illustrate the wide variety of sources, as shown in Fig. 1.1, which can be roughly separated under the general headings of 'point' and 'diffuse' locations, and which are of continuous or intermittent occurrence. The identification of continuous or near-continuous inputs is relatively simple by routine regular water-sampling programmes but sporadic discharges may well go undetected unless a fish kill occurs or the incident is recorded by the more frequent monitoring of a water supply intake. These cases become media headlines; however, there may be many more occurrences which go undetected, because no immediately obvious effects are seen. Alternatively, the timing of the incident may not have coincided with the taking of samples for routine water quality monitoring. This is a major problem in pollution control. One fact which emerges from this description of the various types of input is that the concentrations of man-made chemicals in a water body will never remain constant. Even if there were to be an effluent discharge which remained constant 24 hours a day, seven days a week, the varying dilution in the water body caused by changes in rainfall would cause the concentrations to vary. Discharges of domestic wastes to disposal works are not constant; the flow lessens after midnight and begins to increase at dawn with peak flows in the mid-morning and evening, when most domestic water is used. Over the past two decades the peak discharge of detergents on a Monday morning, when traditionally the week's household laundry was done, has been smoothed out by changes in domestic timetables and the advent of the automatic washing machine. However, there are many industries that use batch processes in the manufacture of their products, and there may be intermittent discharges of spent solutions from such processes to the sewer.

Sediments

Contaminated sediments are another significant source of pollution. These may be derived from inputs of suspended solids to which toxic substances are adsorbed, such as soil particles in surface water run-off from fields treated with pesticides. Alternatively, the natural suspended material in a watercourse as well as the river bed surface can adsorb chemicals from the water. When the suspended material settles out, the toxic material forms a sink or reservoir; the extent to which this can cause harm to aquatic life depends on the strength of the bond between the chemical and the particles. Substances with a very low solubility in water can be tightly bound and persist in the sediment for a long time. However, they may not be available for uptake by organisms in the sediment unless there is a direct route of entry through the skin surface or the gut. Although very low, the toxic inputs derived from the release of contaminants from sediments are likely to continue for a long time at a slow steady rate.

CONCLUSIONS

Rivers and lakes are a very important part of our natural heritage. They have been widely utilized by mankind over the centuries, to the extent that very few, if any, are now in a 'natural' condition. One of the most significant man-made changes has been the addition of chemicals to these waters. Such inputs to water can be derived from a variety of sources, some of them obvious, and others less so. They can be very variable so that the concentrations of chemicals in the water are rarely constant. As industrial, agricultural and domestic practices change, evolve and develop, so the types of chemical inputs, and therefore their importance, will be altered; there will always be new problems that need to be assessed.

In this introduction the term 'pollution' has been used in a very general and descriptive manner. However, if we are to control pollution, then we need to have a clear understanding of what we are trying to prevent. Chapter 2 begins by defining what is meant by 'pollution'.

2 What is Pollution? — Definitions and Effects

Chapter 1 described some of the factors which vary in the freshwater environment, both in terms of the physical characteristics of the rivers and lakes and the chemical composition of the water. None of these factors remain constant; they vary from year to year and from decade to decade. Wet years in which there is substantial run-off from the land, erosion of the bed and banks of watercourses and flooding of adjacent areas, are interspersed with dry periods in which there are low flows, reduced river width and higher temperatures. The animal and plant communities in the water are always in a state of flux, reacting to these changes in their environment.

Today, we are cushioned against the vagaries of our climate by central heating and perhaps air-conditioning; modern agricultural practices and food preservation techniques provide us with a constant year-round supply of food and a varied diet. We tend to forget that natural populations of animals and plants can undergo considerable changes in abundance from year to year in response to fluctuations in climate and in predator-prey relationships. And we tend to expect our environment to remain constant and to regard any deviations as the result of human interference. Too often we overlook the role of climatic changes, especially the frequency and seasonal pattern of rainfall, on the balance of aquatic animal and plant communities.

DEFINITION OF POLLUTION IN RELATION TO WATER USE

How, then, do we define this widely used but emotive term

which has become analogous to 'sin'? What is pollution? Marine pollution has been defined by GESAMP, 1980 as:

'the introduction by man, directly or indirectly, of substances or energy (e.g. heat) into the marine environment (including estuaries) resulting in such deleterious effects as harm to living resources, hazards to human health, hindrance to marine activities including fishing, impairment of quality for use of seawater and reduction of amenities.'

In this definition, the plants and animals that live in the sea are seen as a resource which needs to be conserved. If man's activities have a harmful effect on this resource, then pollution has occurred. No such accepted definition exists for freshwater, but the general concept is transferable between the two environments. Man-made alterations to water-flow-rates are understandably not included in this definition, but the general perception of pollution is that it is caused by substances (e.g. chemicals) and heated effluents.

To put it another way, pollution has occurred when we are prevented from deriving various benefits from our freshwaters because they contain unacceptable levels of chemicals or heat derived from man's activities. These benefits have been defined in the UK as a series of 'uses' (see Water Research Centre reports, References) made of freshwater:

(1) Direct abstraction to potable supply,
(2) Food for human consumption derived from freshwaters,
(3) Protection of freshwater fish,
(4) Protection of aquatic life,
(5) Irrigation of crops,
(6) Livestock watering,
(7) Industrial abstraction for food processing,
(8) Recreational use for bathing and water contact sports,
(9) Aesthetic acceptability.

Some of these uses apply to a limited number of locations in our rivers and lakes; others, such as the protection of

freshwater fish and aquatic life in general, can apply throughout the entire system. Although the subject of this book is the
protection of fish in freshwater from pollution, it is obvious
that these species depend on the availability (and hence the
protection) of other aquatic life for their food if the fishery is
to flourish.

The interactions between man's various activities and the
effect which these have on different components of the aquatic
ecosystem aquatic life are shown in Fig. 2.1. Changes in land
use, the use made of the water and several socio-economic
factors can cause a load to be placed on the aquatic ecosystem.
In this context, the term 'load' is used in an engineering
sense, in that it contributes to the stresses which are placed
on aquatic life. The loading from these changes is over and
above that arising from the natural changes derived from a
variable climate to which the organisms may be able to adapt
to a greater or lesser extent, or which gives rise to changes in
species abundance. Pollution occurs when this additional

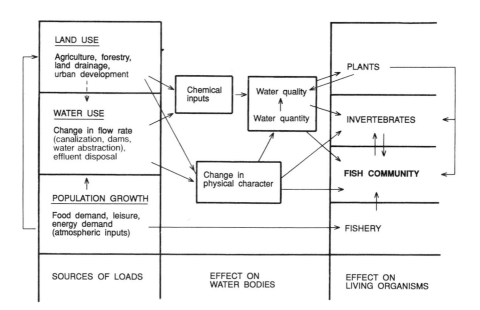

Fig. 2.1 Interrelationships between the major environmental factors which
can affect a fish community.

loading is sufficient to reduce the value of the resource to an unacceptable degree.

UNACCEPTABLE CHANGE

When do the changes caused by man to the aquatic environment become unacceptable? It is clear that any loading over and above the natural load will have an additional effect on the aquatic communities. Indeed, it is these very changes which have been used by aquatic biologists to classify the deterioration of water quality; biological indices have been constructed based on the number and abundance of sensitive and resistant species at sampling sites which provide a quantitative measure of the extra loading. There is no scientifically defined boundary between what changes are unacceptable and what are acceptable; this is a value judgement. However, few would now argue that a river made fishless by the discharge into it of toxic effluents was acceptable. And yet, as pointed out in the previous chapter, this was the accepted condition of many of the rivers draining our industrial cities in the early years of this century. The research programmes which were initiated 60 years ago and which slowly gathered momentum in the succeeding years were designed to answer the question 'What reduction in the pollution load will be required to re-establish a healthy fish community?'. This was the starting point in the calculation of the most cost-effective approach to restoring this particular resource.

THE CONCEPT OF THE ENVIRONMENTAL QUALITY STANDARD (EQS)

The relationship between additional loading and its effect on aquatic life is shown in Fig. 2.2 in order to explain some of the terminology used. Pollution as defined above is caused when the effect of the loading on the resource is unacceptable. The point at which the load of a chemical is sufficiently

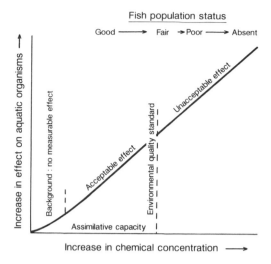

Fig. 2.2 Relationship between increase in chemical inputs and effects on aquatic life.

reduced for the resource to be restored represents the environmental quality standard (EQS) or, more specifically, a water quality standard (WQS) for that substance in the context of a defined water use, also known as the environmental quality objective (EQO) or, more specifically, the water quality objective (WQO).

Water containing concentrations of the chemical which are below this standard are said to be 'contaminated', a term used to indicate that the substances present in the water are at concentrations that are not harmful to the EQO. The use of this term can cause confusion because in other contexts, such as the purity of foodstuffs, this term is associated with harmfulness.

The ability of the resource to withstand a small increase in loading is known as the 'assimilative capacity'. Within this zone, some pollution-sensitive species will be reduced in number or disappear, but this may be acceptable if they do not play a vital role in the aquatic community and are replaced by more resistant species with a similar function within the aquatic ecosystem. Clearly, species that are valued for recreational, commercial or scientific purposes should by definition be unaffected by this small loading, so that such resources remain unimpaired.

This 'top down' approach to pollution control stems from the primary objective of restoring fishless rivers. However, public concern is now beginning to focus on the need to protect clean waters; this is particularly the case in the marine environment where there is no history of severe pollution other than in estuaries.

DEFINITION OF POLLUTION IN RELATION TO INPUTS

The perceived need to protect clean environments has led to an alternative definition of pollution: 'any additional loading by substances or energy as a result of man's activity'. By this definition almost all waters are polluted to a greater or lesser extent, the only difference being in the severity of the pollution in any one area. There is no recognition of an assimilative capacity under this definition and acceptable loadings are expressed as limited increases above the background levels. As the loading increases, the EQS is redefined as the *danger* concentration which should not be exceeded, instead of the *safe* concentration which should be achieved in order to re-establish a fishery. This change in perception of what constitutes pollution represents a swing away from an anthropocentric view, in which man requires protection of the natural resources which he wishes to exploit, towards an ecocentric view, in which the environment itself should be preserved in its totality. In the context of water pollution, the ecocentric view has been more strongly expressed in the marine environment, probably because this is seen as a remaining wilderness (especially in the polar regions) in contrast to the man-made changes to much of the land surface. There may be less public support for an ecocentric definition of pollution in freshwaters because of their long history of utilization for a variety of acceptable purposes but, as will be seen, it is having an influence on pollution control strategy. However, it must be recognized that the existence of two definitions of pollution has caused confusion, and it has led to apparently conflicting statements on the condition of our rivers and lakes.

A problem associated with the second definition is that the sensitivity of chemical analytical techniques has improved enormously in the past few decades. In 1950, 1 ppm was regarded as a low concentration; now, many chemicals can be measured at levels a hundred thousand times lower than this. Therefore, an increasing number of man-made chemicals can be detected and measured in our surface waters and this equates to pollution under the ecocentric definition, even though their concentrations may be so low that the additional loading on the aquatic environment is insignificant. Indeed, we may be entering a period of 'chemophobia' in which the mere presence of measurable concentrations of man-made chemicals in the environment is considered to be unacceptable. In such situations, whether or not surface waters are found to be polluted by such substances is dependent on the sensitivity of the analytical methods available for their detection. This book focuses on the effects of chemicals on fish; although increases in thermal loading can be important, for example, downstream of electricity generating stations, the problems caused are relatively easy to define. Further information on this subject can be found in Alabaster & Lloyd (1982).

PUTTING POLLUTION IN PERSPECTIVE

In Chapter 1 the point was made that few, if any, of our rivers and lakes are in their natural primeval condition because they receive various types of loading, as shown in Fig. 2.1. It does seem illogical that there is a perceived need to afford complete protection from man-made chemicals to the aquatic communities which have developed in these waters, whereas the other types of loading, which have rendered the watercourses 'unnatural', are regarded as acceptable. In the end, however, it is public opinion, translated into political pressure, that determines the relative acceptabilities of these various factors.

HOW CHEMICALS CAN AFFECT FISH

In order to understand the way in which fish can be harmed
by chemicals in the water, it is helpful to know a little about
their basic structure and physiology, especially in relation to
the function of the gills. This is because the gills are directly
exposed to the chemicals that are in the water, in the same
way as the lungs of terrestrial vertebrates are exposed to
atmospheric pollutants. Therefore, fish living in waters containing toxic chemicals can be thought of as living in a polluted 'atmosphere'. Detailed descriptions of fish anatomy and
physiology can be found in standard textbooks on vertebrate
zoology, and the classic work on fish gills is that of Hoar &
Randall (1984).

Osmoregulation

Fish differ from terrestrial organisms in that they have to
maintain an osmotic equilibrium with the surrounding water.
The body fluids in a freshwater fish have a much higher salt
content than that of the surrounding water. Therefore, by
simple osmosis, water is taken up into the body. As in humans,
this water is filtered from the blood by the kidneys but in fish
there is no resorption of water and a copious flow of urine is
produced. Freshwater fish are in no danger of dehydration!
However, the kidneys do resorb much of the sodium and
chloride from the urine in order to prevent undue loss of salt.

Because fish skin is not waterproof, sodium and chloride
escape from the body although the rate at which this occurs
can be slowed up by the layer of mucus on the skin surface.
This salt loss is restored by the active uptake of these elements
via special cells in the gills, where sodium is exchanged for
hydrogen and chloride for bicarbonate. Therefore, in contrast
to man, the major regulation of the salt balance is carried out
by the gills and not by the kidneys. These osmoregulatory
factors are shown in Fig. 2.3. This function of the gills is
just as important as their more commonly known use as a
respiratory organ.

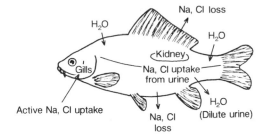

Fig. 2.3 Basic features of osmoregulation in freshwater fish.

Respiration

Fish obtain oxygen from the small amount which is dissolved as gas in the water (not from the oxygen in H_2O!). In order to extract this oxygen efficiently, the gill structure consists of a very fine sieve through which water is pumped by muscular action of the mouth and pharynx. The general structure is shown in Fig. 2.4. The primary lamellae or filaments are attached to the gill arches like teeth on a comb. These lamellae are slightly curved so that their tips meet those of the adjoining

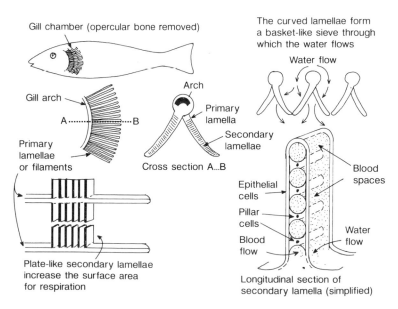

Fig. 2.4 Diagrammatic description of fish gill structure.

gill arch, the whole system forming a folded filter. To increase the efficiency of the filter, there are plate-like secondary lamellae on the upper and lower surface of the branchial lamellae, and the respiratory water has to pass between these plates. The structure of these plates can be compared to a sandwich consisting of a thin layer of epithelial cells on the outside and spaces through which the blood flows on the inside. Therefore, the dissolved oxygen in the water has to cross only a very short distance to get into the blood stream. Added to this, the blood flows in the opposite direction to that of the water and so acts in a similar fashion to a heat exchanger, which increases the efficiency of oxygen extraction still further.

As a result of this arrangement, trout, for example, can extract up to 80% of the oxygen dissolved in the respiratory water. But it is this very same efficiency that makes fish vulnerable to toxic substances in the water.

Uptake of chemicals by fish

Chemicals in the water can be absorbed by the gills, pass into the bloodstream and circulate through the body. Furthermore, if the concentrations of toxic chemicals are high enough, the delicate cells of the gill secondary lamellae can be damaged and this adversely affects the vital functions of respiration and salt regulation. The gills are of primary importance as a route whereby toxic chemicals in the water can be taken up by fish, and in the majority of cases the intake of such substances in the food is of a much lesser secondary importance.

Uptake of small particles

Another route of entry, but about which very little is known, is the uptake of very small particles by the skin and gills. Bacteria can pass between the cells of the surface epithelium and once inside they are normally countered by disease defence mechanisms. However, inert particles of bacterial size can likewise gain entry and in high concentrations may disrupt the defences. It is also possible that such particles with toxic substances on their surface may be even more harmful. If local disease defence mechanisms are weakened, then bacteria can multiply and cause skin ulcers and fin rot. It is obvious that those species of fish which live in contact with sediments will be most at risk from such sources of pollution, especially flatfish in the marine environment. Some protection may be given by the film of mucus which covers the skin and gills, but this may be lost by netting, handling or other abrasive actions and so open the way to chemical attack and/or the entry of disease organisms. Much more research is required to establish whether this route is important for the uptake of harmful substances adsorbed onto microparticulate matter.

Defence mechanisms in the body

Once past the surface epithelium, toxic chemicals can affect any one of a whole range of bodily functions depending on their specific mode of toxic action. In turn, fish have a number of defence mechanisms to prevent such effects occurring; organic chemicals can be detoxified in the liver and their metabolites may be excreted via the bile and the gut. So-called 'heavy metals' such as zinc and cadmium can be attached to special proteins in the blood and may be deposited within insoluble granules which are then stored or excreted.

These defences can be triggered or activated by the presence of the toxic substance and, if its concentration is low, the fish may develop a resistance which enables it to withstand a higher dose that would otherwise be harmful. On the other hand, a prolonged exposure to a toxic substance in the water may exhaust the defence mechanism so that the fish becomes weakened and subsequently may succumb. This short-term adaptation is called 'acclimation', to distinguish it from an increased resistance in a population caused by the natural selection of hardier individuals, which is termed 'acclimatization'. As with the distinction between pollution and contamination, these terms can be confusing but it is necessary to make the distinction between the two types of adaptation.

The system is therefore one of attack and counter-attack. Some of the mechanisms involved will be described in more detail in the following chapters. But the point should be made here that the defences have been developed by fish over millions of years in response to natural loadings on the aquatic environment and these mechanisms have been obviously successful. They have, therefore, a limited capacity to withstand some of the additional loads that arise as a result of man's recent activities. To some extent this capacity derives from the fact that fish, being cold-blooded, have an internal physiology more loosely organized than that of warm-blooded animals, and this flexibility provides a better buffer against changes in the external environment. This is one of the reasons why it is difficult to extrapolate from information on the effects of a chemical on the bodily functions of a warm-blooded mammal to predict or explain effects on cold-blooded fish. Small deviations from normality which may be harmful to the former may be within the acceptable range of the latter.

CONCLUSIONS

The term 'pollution' as applied to water can be defined in either an anthropogenic or an ecocentric manner. This term is often used loosely and can cause confusion. Both definitions of pollution refer to the introduction by man of chemicals into the aquatic environment. The effects caused by such chemicals should be assessed in conjunction with all the other natural and man-made factors that can affect fish populations. Fish live in equilibrium with their surroundings and they can readily adapt to natural changes in the environment; they have a limited capacity to adapt to man-made changes. This forms part of the assimilative capacity of the aquatic environment whereby the impact of limited inputs of chemicals can be absorbed without causing significant damage to fish and other aquatic life.

The following chapters describe the methods that can be used to measure the extent to which fish can withstand an increased chemical load in the water without being harmed.

3 Assessing the Toxicity of Chemicals

So far, the effect of chemicals on fish has been described as a general loading; now it is necessary to consider the way in which their individual toxic actions can be measured. The first important point to remember is that all chemicals are harmful if they are present in high enough concentrations, even those chemicals which are essential to life at lower concentrations. For example, even sodium chloride is toxic to freshwater fish at the levels found in seawater because water is drawn out of the body by osmosis and this leads to dehydration. On the other hand, pure distilled water which contains no salts is lethal to fish because the sodium and chloride which leach from the body cannot then be replaced by their uptake from the water through the gills. A minimum amount of sodium chloride is essential in the water to support fish life.

At low concentrations, chemicals can have a variety of different toxic actions which produce different toxic effects, but at high enough concentrations they have one common effect, that is, they cause the fish to die. Tests are therefore carried out on each chemical to obtain a concentration-response relationship so that the limiting amount of the substance which causes death can be calculated. It is regrettable that mortality has had to be used as the common response of fish to chemicals, and considerable effort is being made to find a lesser effect which is common to all chemicals and which can still be equated with damage to the organism. So far this effort has achieved little success and in the meantime, there are few practical alternatives other than reducing the number of fish used in these tests to the absolute minimum.

The descriptions of the various methods used to obtain concentration-response relationships may be too technical for the non-scientist, but they serve to illustrate some of the complexities of assessing the hazardous properties of chemicals to fish. More detailed descriptions of the methodology can be found in standard works such as those by Rand & Petrocelli (1985) and Abel (1989). A classic work on the design and use of toxicity tests with fish is Sprague (1973), which is a condensed version of three, more detailed, papers (Sprague 1969, 1970, 1971).

STANDARD TOXICITY TESTS

These have been developed to obtain the concentration-response relationship for fish exposed to chemicals. A series of five or six concentrations of a chemical is prepared in water and these solutions are then transferred to aquaria; the concentrations are chosen from the result of a preliminary test with a few fish which establishes the approximate range within which damage begins to occur. Between seven to ten fish are then placed into each aquarium and their survival times are recorded. One aquarium contains clean water with no added chemical in which all the fish are expected to survive. If more than one fish dies in this control aquarium the test is not valid because factors other than the chemical may be affecting the survival of the fish. The times at which individual fish die in each concentration of chemical are recorded.

The survival times of the fish can be used to construct a toxicity curve as shown in Fig. 3.1. This can be done in two ways. The average survival time of each batch of fish can be calculated and these can be plotted against the corresponding concentration on the graph. These are known as the LT_{50}s (the time taken for 50% of the fish to die in each concentration). Also, at fixed times during the test such as 6, 24, 48, 72 and 96 h after the start, the concentration causing 50% mortality can be calculated; these are the LC_{50}s (the concentration

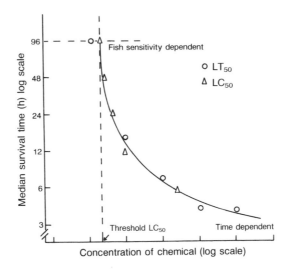

Fig. 3.1 Generalized construction and characteristics of a toxicity curve.

lethal to 50% of the fish at each time interval). These values can then be plotted against the corresponding exposure periods and concentrations on a graph. The details of the statistical methods used can be found in manuals and textbooks on this subject, such as those given earlier in this chapter. For our purposes, it is necessary only to understand the general principles involved in constructing a toxicity curve.

In the early days of fish toxicity testing it was customary to finish the test after 48 h; later, this was extended to 96 h. There was no sound biological reason for the choice of these periods; a 48 h test allowed two tests to be carried out within a 5-day working week, and a 96 h test could be completed within a week and leave the weekend free. As time progressed it became customary, especially in North America, to express the result of the toxicity test as a single value, the 96 h LC_{50} – this being the calculated concentration which would kill 50% of a batch of fish within that time period.

SHAPES OF TOXICITY CURVES

More recently, however, it has become increasingly recognized that a considerable amount of extra information can be obtained from the specific shape of the toxicity curve. At highly toxic concentrations, the toxicity curve is parallel to the concentration axis. This represents the minimum time taken for the substance to produce a harmful effect; for poisons such as hydrogen cyanide this time may be very short, as it is for humans. For other substances which affect less essential processes in the body, this minimum time of reaction may be longer than a day. As shown in Fig. 3.1, this part of the toxicity curve is said to be time dependent, because the survival times change very little with increases in concentration.

With longer exposure times, the curve can become parallel to the time axis. This is because as the concentration of chemical becomes less, so the fish is better able to metabolize, detoxify and excrete the amount entering the body. Ultimately, an equilibrium can be reached when the rate of uptake of the chemical is balanced by the rate of its loss. The concentration at which this equilibrium is reached is called the threshold LC_{50} for those tests that use mortality as the measured harmful effect. This threshold value is independent of time because increases in the exposure period will not change the LC_{50} and so it is a true measure of the sensitivity of the fish to that substance under the conditions of the test. Where a threshold concentration becomes apparent after a few hours (Fig. 3.2,

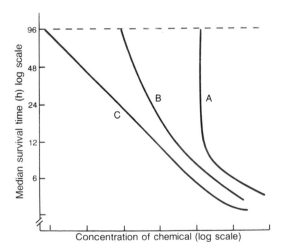

Fig. 3.2 Shapes of toxicity curves.

Curve A), the likely explanation is that the detoxification processes are mobilized rapidly, and those fish which survive in slightly lower concentrations may thereby become more resistant to higher levels of the toxic substance. An example of such a substance is ammonia, the toxicity of which will be described in greater detail in Chapter 5.

Where the detoxification processes within the fish take longer to activate, the toxicity curve may be shallower and the threshold concentration becomes apparent only after an extended exposure period (Fig. 3.2, Curve B). The extreme case (Curve C) is reached by those chemicals such as the pesticide DDT which have a very low solubility in water and are very soluble in fat, that is, they are lipophilic. If they cannot be detoxified by the fish, then even a very slow rate of uptake from the low concentrations in the water can build up gradually in the fatty tissues to a point when a lethal concentration is reached. However, it is likely that a threshold concentration would ultimately be achieved; in very low concentrations the rate of uptake may be so slow that it is matched by the growth rate of the fish, so that the actual concentrations in the tissues do not increase. Also, it would be most unlikely that there would be no loss of the chemical from the tissues. The important point which must be made here is that the threshold concentrations of these substances can only be established in experiments that continue for considerably longer than four days. It follows that the 96 h LC_{50} for such chemicals does not provide a true measure of their comparative harmfulness to fish because this value is still time dependent and, in contrast to other chemicals, does not represent an equilibrium concentration.

The shape of the toxicity curve, therefore, can provide valuable information on the toxic properties of a chemical. Furthermore, the time-dependent portion of the curve can be important in assessing the likely impact of sporadic pollution where high concentrations of a toxic substance are present only for a short period. In these cases it is important to determine whether fish exposed to potentially lethal concentrations for a short period of time (less than that required to produce mortalities as shown on the toxicity curve) will survive when returned to clean water, or whether an irreversible toxic effect occurs in the early stages of exposure and the fish will then eventually die even if returned to clean water. The usual case for chemicals with toxicity curves types A and B (Fig. 3.2) is that exposures of up to half the time required to produce a harmful effect will not cause irreversible damage.

CONSTANT CONCENTRATIONS IN TOXICITY TESTS

An accurate and reproducible toxicity curve can be obtained only if the concentrations of the chemical in the separate aquaria are kept constant, or as near to constant as possible. This may seem easy to achieve but in practice it can pose considerable problems, as shown in Fig. 3.3. Some chemicals such as pesticides which are toxic at very low concentrations

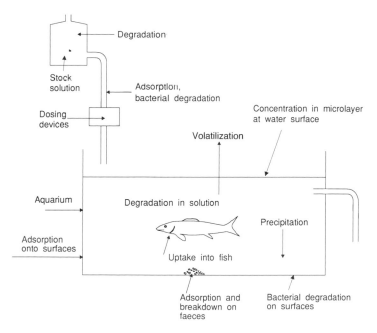

Fig. 3.3 Causes of reduced chemical concentrations in toxicity test solutions.

can be adsorbed onto the walls of the aquaria. Others, such as phenol, can be readily broken down by bacteria in the water. It is obvious that volatile substances such as benzene will be lost to the atmosphere, even if the aquaria are not aerated. The effect of such a gradual reduction in the concentration in the water will be to increase the survival time of the fish and incorrectly indicate the existence of a higher threshold value reached in a shorter time interval. It has been claimed that such an inaccuracy is acceptable because it mimics the situation where a chemical is accidentally discharged into a watercourse and the fish are exposed to an initial high concentration which then becomes gradually diluted. However, unless the gradual loss of the chemical is carefully controlled and is maintained at a constant rate in every aquarium, the results are very difficult to interpret correctly. Also, the results obtained in this way can then only be applied to a field situation where the same rate of loss occurs.

To some extent, the concentrations of chemical in the aquaria can be kept reasonably constant by replacing the water with fresh solutions every day. This also removes the excretory products which could otherwise build up and affect the results of the test. Another method is to maintain a continuous flow of fresh solution through the aquaria, so that chemical loss is kept to a minimum. Several sophisticated designs of such apparatus are available and they have the advantage that if the control of the dilutions can be shown to be accurate and constant, there is no need for chemical analyses to prove that the fish were indeed exposed to the required concentrations for the whole of the test period.

CHEMICALS OF LOW SOLUBILITY IN WATER

Another source of error can occur with chemicals of low solubility. It is not uncommon to read reports of tests where the toxic concentrations quoted exceed the known solubility of the chemical in water. In these cases, the fish may have been exposed to much lower than expected concentrations of chemical in the water with most of the chemical lying as a precipitate on the bottom of the aquarium. This problem can be overcome to some extent by adding very small amounts of relatively low toxicity solvents such as acetone which are miscible with water and which can keep higher concentrations of the chemical in solution. Again, the results of these tests have to be interpreted carefully and the possibility of an extra effect caused by the solvent must be taken into account.

Substances with a low water solubility may become concentrated in the microlayer at the water-air interface. Although this is unlikely to make a significant reduction in the concentration of the test water, it can lead to analytical errors if water samples are taken by dipping a beaker just below the water surface. The use of such analytical data to represent the exposure concentration will produce errors in the construction of the toxicity curve.

DISCUSSION

Every effort has to be made to ensure that the fish are exposed to the required concentrations throughout the entire period of the test. Implicit in this is the requirement that the chemical analysis should measure the actual concentrations to which the fish have been exposed. This is necessary to obtain the true shape of the toxicity curve and also to provide an accurate measure of the LC_{50}s which, by definition, relate to the concentration which the fish were exposed to throughout the stated period, for example 48 or 96 h. Again, it should be stressed that the shape of the toxicity curve must be established in order to show whether the 96 h LC_{50} is a threshold value and thus truly reflects the sensitivity of the fish to the chemical.

The position of a toxicity curve for a chemical on the graph in relation to the time and concentration axes, relates only to the species of fish, and the temperature and the chemical characteristics of the dilution water used in the test. Changes in any of these factors may alter the position of the curve on the graph, either by increasing or decreasing the survival time or the threshold concentration, or both. Those factors that are important in this respect are shown in Fig. 3.4 and they are described in detail in the following sections.

FACTORS THAT AFFECT THE RESULTS OF TOXICITY TESTS

There are a number of physical, chemical and biological factors that can affect the results obtained from toxicity tests; those of major importance are now discussed.

Species of fish

The most commonly used fish for toxicity tests are those which can be readily obtained from a commercial supplier or which can be easily bred in the laboratory. An example of the former is the rainbow trout which is widely farmed in temperate climates and can be readily obtained in a convenient

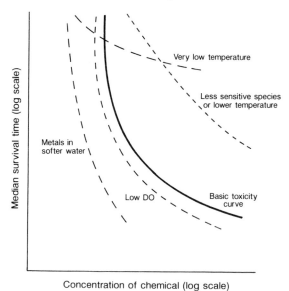

Fig. 3.4 Some factors that change the position of the toxicity curve obtained for fish (e.g. rainbow trout) under standard test conditions.

size range throughout the year, especially now that the breeding season can be extended over several months. There seem
to be no difficulties with different populations or strains
having different sensitivities; for example, toxicity tests with
rainbow trout carried out on a chemical in North America
give the same results as those carried out in Europe, providing
that the test conditions are the same in both cases. Rainbow
trout are active fish and so have a high respiratory rate;
therefore the flow rate of water over the gills is high and thus
the uptake of chemicals from the water will be correspondingly
rapid. Likewise, the general metabolism of the fish tissues is
high, so that detoxification and excretion are also rapid. In
this way the fish quickly reaches an equilibrium with the
chemical in the surrounding water, and a threshold concentration can be established for many chemicals within the 96 h
of a standard toxicity test.

Small, active tropical fish have similar characteristics and
the zebra fish (*Brachydanio rerio*) is the species chosen by
the International Standards Organization for its standard acute
(i.e. short-term) fish toxicity test. It has the additional advantages that it can be bred all the year round in the laboratory
and, because it is smaller than, for example, the rainbow
trout, less water (and less space for the test apparatus) is
required.

At the other extreme are fish such as the goldfish, which
was used in the early days of toxicity testing because of its
ready availability and its general hardiness in captivity. But
this latter characteristic, so necessary for a species kept as a
pet in a small bowl on the window sill, is linked to a low
metabolic rate in cool temperate waters and a general resistance
to chemicals. For this reason they are not now used for
routine toxicity tests at temperatures at or below 15°C because
there is a lesser chance of an equilibrium being reached in
four days, so that the 96 h LC_{50} obtained is not a true measure
of the sensitivity of this fish species. This is not to say that
toxicity tests should be carried out only with more sensitive
species of fish. Obviously, if pollution in a particular area is
being studied, then the effects on the indigenous fish species

there will have to be investigated. But it must be borne in mind that for some species the exposure period to the chemical may need to be extended beyond four days if a threshold concentration is to be established. This is shown in Fig. 3.4 where the toxicity curve for such species is moved upwards and to the right on the graph.

Natural environmental factors

Temperature

Standard toxicity tests are carried out at a constant fixed temperature. However, in natural waters the daily temperature can fluctuate within a 5°C range and on a seasonal basis within the range 0–30°C or even higher. These changes will affect the rate of reaction and possibly the sensitivity of the fish to pollution, as well as the toxic state of some chemicals in the water.

Fish, being cold-blooded, have body temperatures the same as that of the surrounding water. As the temperature changes, the internal physiology of the fish is altered so that it can continue to function efficiently. This is done by replacing enzymes which have a certain efficiency optimum in one temperature range with those which are more efficient at a different optimum temperature. This takes time, which is why fish have to be acclimated slowly when they are transferred from cold to warmer water and vice versa. Maximum acceptable rates of temperature change will vary with the species of fish and the extent to which the new temperature differs from their preferred range. For example, a warm-water fish may take longer to adapt to a low temperature than a cold-water species. As a general rule, however, the temperature change should not exceed 5°C per day within the middle of the range experienced by the fish, and 3°C per day at the extremes. Once the new temperature has been reached, the fish have to be maintained at that condition for several days so that a new internal physiological equilibrium can become established.

Although these changes enable the fish to function more effectively over a wide range of temperatures, the overall rate of their metabolism will still be higher as temperatures increase. Because of this, fish have to be carefully acclimated to temperature when they are used in standard toxicity tests, so that they are in a stable equilibrium and not in a transitional stage where they are under additional stress and therefore perhaps more sensitive to the chemical under test.

The main effect of temperature in a toxicity test is to increase or decrease the time taken for the fish to respond to the chemical. Thus, the toxicity curve will be displaced upwards in colder water because the fish takes longer to react, the toxic mechanisms being slower to take effect. However, over the normal temperature range, the sensitivity of the fish may remain the same when measured in longer term tests and the threshold concentration may be unchanged. This unchanged sensitivity may not be apparent if the tests are terminated at the end of four days, which is another reason why the results of such tests have to be treated with caution.

Nevertheless, the delayed reaction time of fish to chemicals in cold water may be important in determining the effect of accidental discharges of substances to water during the winter months. In such cases, fish may be more able to withstand the effects of short exposures to the chemical than they would if the water was warmer.

There is some evidence to suggest that fish may be more sensitive to chemicals in very cold water, for example below 5°C. This may be because the efficiency of their detoxification mechanisms is reduced under these conditions, and so the threshold concentrations are lowered. These twin effects of temperature on the toxicity curve are shown in Fig. 3.4. However, comparatively few experiments have been designed to investigate the effects of low temperatures on the sensitivity of fish to chemicals, probably because of technical problems in achieving such conditions in the laboratory. This is a serious omission because in natural surface waters such temperatures may exist for a considerable time during the winter months.

Another effect of a change in temperature is on the toxic form of some chemicals, particularly those which exist in one or more ionized forms of differing toxicity in water and where the ratio of these forms can change with temperature. Aluminium is one such chemical. Also, there are compounds such as ammonia which can be present in water as the ionized and non-ionized form. In the case of ammonia, the proportion of the toxic non-ionized form is controlled to some extent by the temperature. This aspect of the problem will be explained in greater detail in Chapter 5.

Dissolved oxygen

Normally, natural waters are saturated with dissolved oxygen (DO) in equilibrium with air. The concentration at these saturation values decreases as the temperature of the water rises. Therefore, as the metabolic rate of fish also increases with temperature, water has to be pumped through the gills at a faster rate to supply the fish with the oxygen which it requires. As a result of this, toxic chemicals may come into contact with the gills at an increased rate, so that greater amounts enter the body within a given period of time. However, this may be counteracted by a greater rate of detoxification of the chemical at higher temperatures, so the overall effect of such changes in DO on the sensitivity of the fish may be very small.

However, the DO content of the water can be reduced by other natural factors. Perhaps the most common of these is the respiration of aquatic plants. This comes as a surprise to many people who think of plants as suppliers of oxygen to the water. Plants do this, however, only during the daylight hours when producing carbohydrate from carbon dioxide and water by the process known as photosynthesis and thereby releasing oxygen at a faster rate than that required for respiration. At night, plants only respire: oxygen is absorbed from the water to such an extent that in heavily weeded ponds the concentration can fall to very low levels. This is why fish kills sometimes occur in ponds during the late summer and autumn; the plants are beginning to die back and decompose, and are not producing sufficient oxygen during the day to counteract the oxygen demand for respiration and decomposition during the hours of darkness. Dissolved oxygen levels may be at their lowest in the early morning hours after a warm day with a heavily overcast sky which limits photosynthetic activity; this is when fish mortalities often occur.

It is obvious that these natural events will be exacerbated by discharges of biodegradable material to the water, or by an increase in the concentration of nutrients which may have stimulated excessive plant growth and which subsequently leads to a mass of decaying vegetation.

Apart from the direct effects of low levels of DO on fish — Chapter 5 will consider this in greater detail — the sensitivity of fish to chemicals is also increased. This is important in toxicity tests where the concentration of DO can fall as a result of insufficient aeration of the water to meet the respiratory demands of the fish or perhaps when the chemical tested can be oxidized by bacteria in the water. The effect of lowered oxygen levels is to move the toxicity curve towards lower concentrations, as shown in Fig. 3.4. Because, in contrast to the effect of temperature, the metabolic rate of the fish is relatively unchanged (unless very low, harmful, levels are reached) the threshold toxic concentration is lowered as a result of the increased respiratory rate. A similar effect can be caused by increased fish activity; the increased respiration rate brings additional amounts of dissolved toxic substances into contact with the gill surfaces where they can be absorbed into the body.

Acidity and alkalinity (pH)
The effect of temperature on the toxicity of chemicals which can be present in water in different ionic and non-ionic forms has been briefly described above. But the pH of the water is the main driving force in controlling the relative proportions of the different forms present. For example, ammonia is present in water as the ionized form NH_4^+ and the non-ionized form NH_3. The latter is the more toxic form, and its proportion increases as the water becomes more alkaline. Thus, the toxicity of a given concentration of ammonia increases ten-fold with an increase in pH from 7.0 to 8.0, because the proportion of

the toxic non-ionized form in the solution increases by that
amount.

For this reason, the pH of the water used in toxicity tests
with substances which ionize has to be controlled within
very narrow limits; for research purposes the variation should
not exceed ±0.05 of a pH unit.

The pH of natural waters is mainly controlled by the buffering action of calcium bicarbonate. Soft acid waters contain
little bicarbonate whereas hard alkaline waters are bicarbonate
rich. Although the bicarbonate concentration of spring waters
arising from underground limestone or chalk sources may
remain relatively unchanged throughout the year, the concentration in other surface waters may vary with the rainfall.
Thus, the pH of the water will fall after heavy rain as the
bicarbonate leached from the soil becomes diluted. It should
be noted here that heavy rain falling on moorland after a
period of drought can flush out stagnant peat bogs which
have become acid, and the subsequent pH of the water may
be sufficiently low to cause fish mortalities.

The pH of bicarbonate-buffered water is also dependent on
the concentration of carbon dioxide present; an increase in
the concentration of this gas will make the water more acid
(as happens with carbonated mineral water). Normally, the
levels present in the water reflect the concentration in the air,
but they can rise if organic matter in the water is being
degraded by bacteria and the oxygen consumed is replaced
by respired carbon dioxide. Thus, low levels of dissolved
oxygen in the water are usually accompanied by higher than
normal concentrations of carbon dioxide.

On the other hand, the active photosynthesis of aquatic
plants removes carbon dioxide from the water, causing the
pH to rise. In extreme conditions of hot sunny weather, a
heavy weed or algal growth in the water, and a moderate
bicarbonate concentration, the pH may rise above 10 by the
afternoon and this can be lethal to fish. It should be noted
that, because this high pH is caused by vigorous photosynthetic
activity, the concentration of DO at this time will be well
above the air saturation value.

Water hardness and humic acids

In addition to other effects described above, calcium has an important influence on the toxicity of metals such as copper, zinc and lead. This is partly due to their competition for uptake into the fish at the gill surface. Therefore, the toxicity of these metals (known as the heavy metals) is greatest in soft acid waters; it is here, too, that the highest concentrations can be found, particularly in those areas of present or past mining activity, where rain can leach toxic metals from spoil heaps and tailing ponds.

However, soft peaty water contains humic acids (which give it a brown colour) and these form soluble complexes with some heavy metals, particularly copper, and thereby reduce their toxicity. Other organic matter such as that found in sewage effluents has the same property. In these circumstances the toxicity exerted by the heavy metals is due mainly to the free uncomplexed ions and not to the total dissolved metal present. These factors have to be taken into account when preparing water for toxicity tests with heavy metals.

Suspended solids

Surface waters normally contain small concentrations of suspended material of organic or mineral origin. These are not harmful to fish; indeed, they can reduce the toxicity of the water by adsorbing chemicals onto their surface. This is particularly important with chemicals of very low water solubility such as organochlorine pesticides. Methods of chemical analysis that measure the total amount of these substances in water can provide misleading predictions of the toxicity if the precipitated or adsorbed material is not available to the fish. This is the same problem as that shown in Fig. 3.3.

CONCLUSIONS

This chapter has re-emphasized a point made in Chapter 1: that the chemical composition of water is variable and that these variations can be on a daily or a seasonal basis. Some of

Table 3.1 Some natural factors that can modify the toxicity of chemicals to fish.

Factor	Modification
Temperature	Controls the rate of response to toxic concentrations Increases toxicity at low temperature? Affects the ionization of some substances (e.g. ammonia)
Dissolved oxygen (DO)	Reduced DO causes increased toxicity
pH	Controls the chemical species present (e.g. aluminium) or degree of ionization (e.g. ammonia)
Hardness (calcium carbonate)	Reduces the toxicity of divalent heavy metals
Humic acids	Forms low toxicity complexes with some metals
Chloride	Reduces toxicity of nitrite
Suspended particulate matter	Adsorbs some chemicals

the changes — for example, those in the temperature and the DO content of the water — will affect the resistance of fish to toxic chemicals; also, changes in temperature, pH, water hardness and humic acids, can affect the toxic state of some chemicals or compete with their uptake by fish. These examples are well known and commonly occur; other examples are less common or only affect a single chemical. (For example, an increase in the chloride content of the water will give fish an added protection against nitrite toxicity). But they serve to emphasize the fact that changes in water composition can alter the position of the toxicity curve, as shown in Fig. 3.4. These effects are summarized in Table 3.1. Data on the toxicity of chemicals to fish should always be accompanied by information on those relevant constituents of the dilution water to which the fish were exposed; if they are not given, then the extent to which the results are appropriate to specific field situations is uncertain.

4 Sub-lethal Tests with Fish

The strong emphasis on toxicity tests which use the mortality of fish as a measure of their response to a chemical probably stems from the time when the main concern was to rehabilitate rivers made fishless by pollution. Information was needed on the concentrations of chemicals that would allow fish to live, so that pollution control measures could be taken to ensure that these levels were not exceeded. However, over the past decades it has been recognized that mere survival may not be sufficient to allow the development of a healthy fish population, and that other harmful effects such as reduced breeding success or the avoidance by fish of polluted water may be important. To some extent, the need for this research was supported by the discovery that persistent pesticides could produce harmful effects at concentrations well below the acute lethal levels (this overlooked the fact that the 96 h LC_{50}s were not threshold values and therefore such effects would have been expected with longer exposure to lower levels). Also, the regulations that control the conduct of experiments with vertebrate animals are becoming more rigorous and the need for tests that cause pain is increasingly questioned on humane grounds. While there is no doubt that this trend is right and proper, difficulties have arisen in finding alternative tests that give comparable unequivocal results. Some of the problems encountered are described in the following Sections; more detailed descriptions are given in the references cited in Chapter 3.

LEVELS OF BIOLOGICAL ORGANIZATION

Measurement of the effects of chemicals on fish can be made at what are known as different levels of organization. The lowest end of the scale is represented by cellular functions within the body and the highest can be represented by a community composed of populations of different fish species. This scale is shown in Fig. 4.1; in between the two extremes are the organizational levels of tissues and organs, the whole body, and a population of one species. There are many different types of reactions or responses which can be measured within each level of organization. For example, there is a vast number of chemical reactions that occur within each cell; there are many types of cell which make up specific tissues and organs; and there are many such structures within the body of the fish. Furthermore, a fish population comprises individuals which themselves are at various life stages which may have different sensitivities to pollution. The community is composed of a number of species which may have different sensitivities to different chemicals.

Clearly, all the interactions at each level, and between each level of organization, are very complex and it would take an enormous amount of research to unravel the various inter-

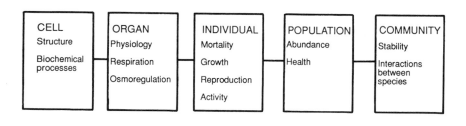

Fig. 4.1 Processes that can be affected by chemicals at different levels of biological organization, with reference to fish (modified from Haux & Forlin 1988).

linking pathways that are involved. At best, our knowledge is only partial, and it is likely to remain so unless the amount of effort expended approaches that devoted to comparable medical research. This has not, of course, deterred those engaged in research on the effects of chemicals at different levels of biological organization, but it is clear that the results obtained from such experiments have to be interpreted with extreme caution.

The cellular level

Because toxic substances exert their harmful effects by interfering with normal chemical reactions within the body, the primary site of action will be within the cell. There are two ways by which such effects can be measured:

(1) Direct measurements can be made on the concentration of various chemicals which can affect the vital processes within the cell, such as enzymes and the substrates on which they act. This can give an insight into the mode of toxic action; for example the inhibition of acetyl cholinesterase in nerve cells by organophosphorous insecticides prevents the normal transmission of electrical impulses.

(2) Other reactions measured may be connected with the detoxification mechanism for a particular chemical. For example, metals such as copper, zinc and cadmium are transported in the blood throughout the body by protein molecules known as metallothioneins. Exposure of a fish to these metals in the water leads to an increase in the body levels of metallothioneins in order to remove them from the gills via the blood to sites where they can be safely stored or excreted. Therefore, metallothionein analysis can be used to determine whether fish have been exposed to higher levels of heavy metals in the environment. Another technique is the measurement of enzymes known as multifunctional oxygenases (MFOs) that are responsible for the breakdown of organic molecules within

the cell. Certain MFOs can break down organic pollutants, and increases in the level of these enzymes can indicate that a fish has been exposed to such chemicals in the water.

Interpretation of the above data requires considerable caution. There is a general tendency to regard any deviation of such responses from normal as being harmful, on the grounds that it adds a small but significant load to the well-being of the fish and that over a period of time this will reduce its chance of survival. On the other hand, it can be argued that once a detoxification mechanism has been developed, and if this can be maintained for as long as the fish is exposed to the particular chemical, then the harmful effects will be minimal. It is possible to envisage a condition where, for example, a starving fish could be so short of energy that the extra small amount required to detoxify chemicals in the body becomes 'the last straw which breaks the camel's back'. However, the chances of a fish surviving in such a weakened state would, anyway, be slim.

It is important, therefore, to distinguish between those effects in a fish that represent an adaptation to an increase in the concentration of chemicals in the water and those effects that reflect a potentially fatal malfunctioning of the body. This scale of effects is shown diagrammatically in Fig. 4.2, with adaptation to chemicals at the lower end and ultimate death at the upper end. This Figure has similarities with Fig. 2.2, Chapter 2, which illustrates the effect of chemicals on populations; a similar type of cause-effect relationship applies to all levels of biological organization. Despite these similarities, it is difficult to extrapolate from the observed effect of a chemical at the cellular level in order to predict whether damage would be caused at the higher levels of organization, and therefore to assess whether this effect on the cells is harmful in terms of the survival of the individual or the population.

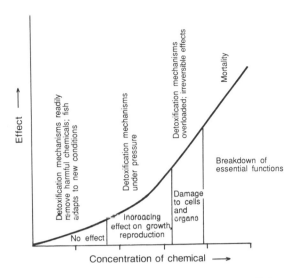

Fig. 4.2 Effects of increasing chemical concentration on fish.

Histopathology
Another important technique for examining effects at the cellular level is histopathology — the microscopical examination of changes in cell structure. Understandably, the effect of chemicals in the water on the cells in fish gills has received considerable attention because primary contact occurs in these cells. Observed effects include the swelling and sometimes the proliferation of the epithelial cells — and heavy metal toxicity can eventually cause these cells to disintegrate. Also, the epithelial layer of cells may lift away from the underlying tissue, thus increasing the thickness of the secondary lamellae. Such effects are damaging to the respiratory and osmoregulatory activity of the fish and the results of extensive research suggest that many chemicals, when present in the water at acutely toxic concentrations, cause this type of damage.

However, recent research (Speare & Ferguson 1989) has shown that these effects may be associated with the process of mortality and not caused by the direct action of the chemical. It was found that fish which were not exposed to pollution but were physically killed and then left in the water for a very short time showed the same type of damage to their gills. This demonstrates one of the main problems in this type of research — separating the specific effects caused by a chemical which lead to death, from the effects which are secondary to the primary damage which has been caused elsewhere in the body.

One of the major changes in gill structure that can reflect a change in water quality concerns the relative proportion of certain cell types present — for example, increases in the abundance of the cells responsible for the excretion of mucus or the uptake of chloride (associated with the maintenance of osmoregulation) in relation to other types of epithelial cells.

Another important use of histopathology is in the identification of abnormal cells (e.g. tumours) in fish exposed to carcinogenic chemicals. These can occur in the liver as well as in other organs where they can be readily identified. It is possible that cold-blooded fish have a wider range of cellular variation which can be regarded as normal than that found in warm-blooded mammals where most of the experience of histopathology has been gained. So in general the main problem is in making the distinction between what is a harmless proliferation of cells and what is potentially harmful. The same problem occurs in the use of certain blood characteristics as a measure of fish health; whereas in a healthy man the concentration of red blood cells remains within a narrow range, in fish the range can be considerable and this may be correlated with the respiratory requirements for different levels of activity and with seasonality. As shown later in Chapter 5, the red blood cell concentration can be rapidly increased in fish undergoing respiratory stress.

Interpretation of results

In conclusion, care must be taken in the interpretation of results of cellular level experiments, and particularly in their extrapolation to predict harmful effects on the whole fish. Perhaps the main value of such studies is to identify the *method* of toxic action of chemicals, and this will be considered further in Chapter 7. Even here, however, the problem remains of distinguishing between a primary effect of a chemical, and a secondary effect.

The organ level

Under this heading are grouped the various vital physiological activities such as respiration and osmoregulation. Again, attention has been focused on gill functions because of their close contact with the chemicals present in the surrounding water.

Respiration
Early research on the effects of pollution on fish respiration used the frequency of opercular movement (which can be easily counted) as a measure of the respiratory rate. Similarly, the 'cough' rate (when the flow of water over the gills is reversed) was recorded as a measure of the irritation caused by the chemical to the gill tissues. Later, measurements were made of the heart-beat rate by means of electrodes which picked up the electrical impulses from the cardiac nerves. All these functions seem to be increased when toxic chemicals are added to the water, and this has been used in the development of 'fish monitors' for the intakes to water-treatment works, in which trout in aquaria are continuously exposed to water drawn from the river and their reactions are monitored to give an early warning of pollution incidents arising from spills upstream. However, the interpretation of such data in terms of fish health is difficult. An increase in oxygen consumption may be associated with additional energy requirements for detoxification, but it is more likely to be caused by the extra activity necessary for an avoidance reaction to the chemical and an attempted escape from the polluted stretch of water.

Osmoregulation
The other important function of the gills is to control the salt content of the body fluids, as outlined in Chapter 2. Special cells regulate the active uptake of sodium and chloride and the excretion of hydrogen and bicarbonate ions. These activities can be disrupted by those chemicals such as zinc and copper which have a direct effect on proteins in the cells.

Also, some chemicals such as ammonia can apparently increase the rate at which water enters the fish, leading to an increase in urine flow as the extra water is pumped out through the kidneys. It is possible that these effects on osmoregulation may be caused by a disruption of the joints between the cells of the gill epithelium, thus making this sheet of tissue less waterproof. However, the concentrations of chemicals that have such a disruptive effect are probably close to, if not exceeding, those that are above the threshold LC_{50}.

These are just some examples of tests at the organ level. In general, they are few in number because the emphasis has been directed either towards the cellular level within the tissue or towards the reaction of whole fish to the chemical.

The whole body level

Tests at this level have been based mainly on two responses:

(1) The energy balance and growth rate of the fish,
(2) The fish's behavioural responses when exposed to chemicals in the water.

Energy balance

The nutrients obtained by fish from their food can be allocated to a number of different functions, as shown in Fig. 4.3 (a model which is, incidentally, applicable to all animals). A proportion must be used to provide energy for basic metabolism, which includes respiration (together with blood circulation), and osmoregulation. The remainder can be allocated between the three main 'scopes' — activity, growth and reproduction — the relative distribution depending in part on the life-style of the fish. Obviously, the proportion of energy allocated to activity will be greater for a mid-water species living in a fast-flowing river than for a bottom-living species in a pond. Activity may be necessary to avoid predators, but rapid growth also enables the fish to reduce the risk of pre-

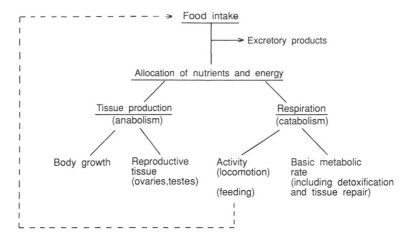

Fig. 4.3 Allocation of energy obtained from the food intake of fish.

dation by larger animals. A rapid growth rate can also be accompanied by an increase in the size of the ovaries in females, so that a greater number of eggs can be produced in order to ensure the survival of the species.

Chemical pollution of the water can affect this balance in several ways. A reduction may occur in the amount of food available or the feeding rate of the fish can be diminished, thus lowering the amount of energy available for allocation to activity and growth. Also, a small amount of energy will be required for detoxification of the chemical. On the other hand, the pollution may be associated with additional nutrients, either directly as with food particles contained in sewage effluents or indirectly as with a general increase in the nutritional status (eutrophication) of the water. In this case, the amount of food available to the fish may be increased and the energy balance improved.

These are complex interactions, and laboratory experiments can only provide information on a limited fraction of the whole spectrum. In the 1960s attempts were made to measure the effects of chemicals on the maximum sustainable swimming speeds of fish. However, the reductions measured were probably due more to the direct effects of the chemical on the ability of the gills to extract oxygen from the water than on the extent to which the energy reserves could be allocated to these activities.

Growth rate

More recently, attention has been directed towards the effect of chemicals on fish growth. Originally these tests were extended to cover the whole life cycle, so that effects on growth, fecundity and the viability of the second generation could be measured. However, such tests were time-consuming and therefore expensive; in practice they could be carried out as a routine only on warm-water fish with a very short life cycle because cold-water species such as trout take at least a year to reach sexual maturity. The disadvantage of these lengthy tests is that the chance of equipment breakdown at some stage is considerable, and a premature end to several months of patient work can be disheartening as well as expensive.

Nevertheless, those tests that were carried out successfully indicated that the most sensitive life-stage was the transition from the embryo to the larval fish, and subsequently a number of standard tests have been developed along these lines. One interesting feature of such tests is that at the outset the embryo is dependent on the food in its yolk sac for energy so that the effects of a toxic chemical on the external food supply or feeding rate is immaterial at this stage. But the transition to external feeding once the yolk has been completely absorbed is a very sensitive period in a fish's life history, as every trout breeder knows, and it is here that low concentrations of chemicals can be harmful – especially if the developing embryo has had to utilize some of its fixed energy supply for the detoxification of chemicals or for the repair of tissue damage. These tests, once standardized, can be reasonably reproducible because the general level of physical activity at this stage of the life cycle is low and probably takes only a small proportion of the available energy.

An alternative approach is to measure the growth rates of juvenile fish exposed to chemicals. In this case the fish have to be supplied with a fixed ration of food, and each individual is cold-branded so that its weight increments can be measured separately. A reduced growth rate can be caused either by a lower feeding rate, or an increased activity associated with an attempt to avoid the contaminated water, or an increased expenditure of energy on chemical detoxification and tissue repair. Again, however, the results from such laboratory tests need to interpreted with care.

One problem is that the normal activity levels of batches of fish in aquaria can vary; sometimes a dominant, aggressive fish can increase the activity of the others, and cause a reduction in their growth rate as well as an increase in their sensitivity to pollutants (Chapter 3). Since the criterion of such tests is to establish the maximum concentration of chemical at which the growth rate of the fish does not differ significantly from those in clean water, such variability in behaviour can reduce the precision and therefore the reproducibility of the test. On the other hand, it can be argued that such variations occur in nature and therefore the tests are not unrealistic. However, the use of 'unnatural' food such as trout pellets and the method of food presentation may affect the behavioural patterns of feeding; a stronger stimulus to feed in the natural environment may be less affected by low concentrations of chemical in the water.

Behaviour
The other main whole body response — avoidance by fish of polluted water — received considerable attention in the early days of fish ecotoxicology. The simplest apparatus for measuring this consisted of a long tube with water inputs at each end and a central drain pipe as shown in Fig. 4.4. A chemical could be introduced into the water supply at one end and this would contaminate one half of the tube. One or more fish were placed in the tube and the length of time spent at each end was recorded. The end at which the chemical was introduced was changed at intervals to allow for the possibility that the fish had a natural preference for one side of the central dividing line. These tests, and more sophisticated versions of them (e.g. a 'Y' shaped configuration simulating a clean and a polluted tributary, and the downstream mixture

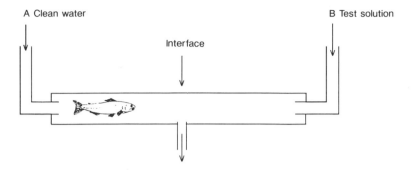

A and B can be reversed, to allow for a preference by the fish
for a particular end of the tank.

Fig. 4.4 A simple apparatus to measure the avoidance reaction of fish to
chemicals.

of the two), presented the fish with a choice between clean
and contaminated water with a sharp interface between the
two conditions. No other incentives were provided although,
in some experiments, a degree of cover to provide darkness
was provided to make one part of the tube more attractive as
a refuge.

Tests of this type provide information on the ability of fish
to detect concentrations of chemicals in the water by measuring
the creatures' observed response in avoiding them. Fish might
be able to detect lower concentrations but might not react to
them by avoidance. Habituation by the fish to the chemical in
the water is rarely taken into account, nor are other factors
such as territorial or migratory behaviour which might have
an overriding effect in the natural environment. For example,
a laboratory experiment showed that when roach were exposed
to a progressive reduction in the DO content in the water,
they remained in their 'home range' until the level became
close to lethal, and only then did they move downstream.
Thereafter, occasional forays were made upstream and when
the DO levels were raised the fish returned to their original
station (Stott & Cross 1973).

Similarly, field observations showed that salmon migrating
upstream to their spawning grounds turned back only when
the levels of copper and zinc (derived from upstream mining

activities) reached near-lethal concentrations (Saunders & Sprague 1967). Much lower concentrations were clearly avoided in simple laboratory tests. It is very likely that the reactions of fish to a slowly increasing level of chemical extending over a long stretch of river will be different from that displayed in a simple laboratory tube where there is a sharp interface between clean and contaminated water. Not all chemicals can be detected and avoided by fish; there are cases where lethal concentrations appear to have an attractive effect, and others where no concentrations produce a reaction.

Another approach to using behavioural responses of fish to chemicals is to record their appearance and activity in the test aquaria. Overturning was commonly used in the past; with some chemicals, such as those having an anaesthetic action, fish that have turned over on to their backs will recover when placed in clean water. With other chemicals, such as the toxic metals, overturning is generally followed by death. Other reactions recorded have been change of colour (darkening or more rarely becoming lighter), swimming at the surface or resting on the aquarium floor, and erratic swimming movements. Subtle changes in behaviour are difficult to record with any accuracy because much depends on the experience of the observer in recognizing normal and abnormal behaviour patterns. But in general it is useful to have such effects re-corded in standard toxicity tests because they do give some indication of effects, whether harmful or not, caused by sub-lethal concentrations. Although dramatic effects such as overturning and swimming at the surface could make fish more liable to predation and can therefore be regarded as harmful, less obvious changes in behaviour are more difficult to interpret in terms of fish survival.

Interpretation of data

These effects on fish energetics, growth and behaviour, are the ones commonly used in sub-lethal toxicity tests, and they both have a clear potential for providing a prediction of the harmful properties of a chemical present in a watercourse. But it is equally clear that the information gained by such toxicity tests must be interpreted with caution and must take into account the extent to which the conditions of the laboratory experiment differ from those that exist in the field.

Susceptibility to disease
It is tempting to suppose that fish that have been weakened by pollution will be more susceptible to disease. However, evidence for such an association is not clear-cut. For example, correlations between the incidence of epidermal diseases in marine flatfish with sources of pollution have not proved that such an association exists. Disease epidemics such as ulcerative dermal necrosis (UDN) of salmon, and roach ulcer disease in recent years were not associated with identifiable pollution. Outbreaks of disease in fish farms are usually associated with high temperature or overcrowding. It is possible that some chemicals at low concentrations will weaken the defences of fish against disease, but it is clear that this is not a common property of pollutants.

However, there is evidence that the presence of significant carcinogenic chemicals in the water will cause tissue abnormalities, especially in the liver, but such examples are confined to areas which are heavily polluted by these substances.

Population and community levels

Although laboratory experiments are normally carried out with a sufficient number of fish to represent a sub-sample of a much larger population of the test species, this only allows for differences in sensitivity between individuals to the chemical and not to any other interactions which can occur between species in natural situations. These interactions can be measured only in model ecosystems. A number of such models have been developed, ranging from simple laboratory tests in which the interactions between a few species representing a food chain are examined (e.g. algae — herbivorous zooplankton — fish), to the use of artificial ponds and streams with a natural assemblage of animals and plants that simulate the natural environment as far as possible.

Experimental ponds

The advantages of the simpler tests are that factors such as the transfer of chemicals through the food chain can be examined together with other behavioural responses which may affect the rates of predation within the food chain. As the tests become more complex, more interactions can be included, but the very complexity of the system then makes it more difficult to control. For example, an experimental design may consist of a series of 12 ponds which at the outset contained as near as possible an identical assemblage of plants and animals. Nine ponds are treated with a chemical, three at a low concentration, three at a medium concentration and three at a high concentration; three are not treated and they act as a control. Samples of fish, invertebrates and algae are taken, sorted and counted so that the effects of the chemical on the various interrelationships can be measured. However, it is impossible to start with identical conditions in each pond and over the course of a few weeks, the community in each pond will develop in different ways, depending on which species achieves an initial dominance. Within small enclosures in which there is no emigration of abundant organisms or immigration of new ones, the dominance of a few species can be accentuated. The use of replicate ponds at each concentration allows for some account to be taken of such natural variability in the development of different communities, but it is possible that subtle effects caused by the chemical will not be distinguishable from the natural variability that occurs between the ponds. Indeed, it is the general experience that only large, dramatic effects can be attributable to the presence of a chemical; for example, synthetic pyrethroid insecticides can have a lethal effect on the zooplankton which then enables a rapid increase in the abundance of algae on which they feed, and this algal bloom can then be harmful to fish (Crossland 1982). Lesser effects, such as changes in the species composition of zooplankton, are more difficult to attribute to the toxic action of a chemical rather than to natural events.

Tests of this type are useful for simulating those conditions where there is a single addition of chemical to the water, such as the accidental overspray or spillage of a pesticide. In these cases there is a subsequent steady reduction in concentration of the chemical in the water; some is accumulated into the sediment, some adsorbed onto plants, and some degraded by bacteria or by chemical and physical reactions in the water. If information is required on the effects of a continuous exposure of organisms to constant concentrations of a chemical, then frequent analyses of the water are required and appropriate additions have to be made to make up for the losses. Even so, there may well be a steady accumulation of chemical in the sediment which will affect the bottom-dwelling organisms. Variations in the way in which the chemical is distributed and lost can have a significant effect on the outcome of the experiment.

Artificial streams
An alternative approach which overcomes some of the problems outlined above is to use artificial streams. These have the advantage that a continuous supply of organisms from a common source can be added to the upstream part of each stream, and any excessive development of any one species within the system is suppressed by emigration downstream and out of the experimental area. Also, the chemical can be continuously dosed into the water to maintain constant concentrations although build-up in the sediments may still be a problem with some chemicals. But these systems are a reasonable representation of a river receiving a continuous discharge of a chemical, and effects on phenomena such as rates of invertebrate drift downstream can be recorded. The main drawback is that a large volume of water is required for even a modest size of stream and this means that a large quantity of chemical is necessary to maintain the desired concentrations. This may be very expensive; also, it may be difficult to dispose of a large volume of polluted water unless

a treatment plant can be installed downstream of the experimental site. Recirculation of the water can overcome the
chemical problems but it could allow the development of
dominant species, as can occur in pond experiments.

Value and limitations of such experiments
Although tests of the type we have been discussing are the
nearest approach to environmental reality, and little extrapolation of the data obtained is necessary to determine the
limiting concentrations of a chemical which causes harm to
aquatic communities, their main drawback is that they are
very time-consuming and therefore very expensive. From a
biological point of view, it may be more cost-effective to
carry out laboratory tests with a wide range of species and to
predict the effects arising from harm caused to any one of
them. Indeed, the major effects recorded in some pond experiments could have been easily predicted from the known
sensitivity of some key organisms to the chemical. This is
especially the case with organic chemicals that have a physical
toxic action and for which there is a narrow range of species
sensitivity. But there is always uncertainty as to whether a
relevant key organism has been overlooked, especially with
pesticides for which there is a wider range of species sensitivity; the use of a multi-species community in a test goes
some way towards overcoming this problem. Also, the cost of
the necessary chemical analyses may well be an overriding
factor in deciding whether such a test should be carried out,
particularly if samples of sediment and organisms as well as
water have to be analysed at frequent intervals. But such
analyses are essential for measuring the actual concentrations
of chemical to which the fish and other organisms have been
exposed. Without this information the value of the biological
measurements is considerably diminished because the results
cannot be used for extrapolation to predict the effects of
concentrations of the chemical in other field situations.

The other point which cannot be stressed too strongly is
that these experiments should be designed so that they can
be repeated by other scientists in order to confirm or question

the results obtained. Therefore, in pond tests the rate of chemical loss from the water and build-up in the sediment must be accurately recorded because the biological results obtained depend on these concentrations; a different rate of chemical redistribution and loss may produce different effects. Similarly, the concentrations of chemical in an experimental stream must be kept constant because this is the only real reproducible condition; the results of an experiment in which the concentrations were allowed to vary widely are really relevant only to those other situations where these same conditions occur, and these may be few in number or even unique.

However, we are reminded in this and previous chapters, that the environment is not in a stable, steady state. We have been discussing complex long-term experiments which measure the subtle sub-lethal effects on fish caused by exposure to constant concentrations of chemicals. How are the results of such experiments relevant to the real world where the environment is in a constant state of change? This is an issue that will be considered in later chapters.

Finally, to what extent does the community of aquatic organisms in the experimental system have to change before harm is considered to have occurred? Disasters such as the elimination of a substantial proportion of the invertebrate zooplankton and the subsequent explosion of algal populations are clearly harmful. But what if a sensitive copepod species is replaced by a more resistant organism which occupies a similar ecological niche? In this case, the general balance of organisms within the ecosystem remains unchanged and only a skilled taxonomist might be able to discover that a change had occurred. Indeed, the extent of the change may be within the natural variation of similar communities found elsewhere. It is clear that when a valued species such as a rare organism is lost then this small change becomes unacceptable. For example, the loss of a rare species of dragonfly unique to a particular area would be more important than the local loss of a common species of midge. At a higher level, a reduction in the numbers of commercially or recreationally important species of fish is more unacceptable to man than a loss of less valued species. It is difficult to quantify and evaluate the damage caused by such changes and it is only recently that environmental economists have begun to address this problem. This subject will be considered again in Chapter 9.

Bioaccumulation of chemicals from the water and through the food chain

It is appropriate at this stage to consider the problem of the accumulation of chemicals in fish, because this is linked to the distribution of such substances in water, sediments and food organisms. Metals such as cadmium and mercury can enter fish by way of the gills or through the food chain, and they can accumulate in various organs, particularly the kidneys, as organometallic compounds or as solid granules in association with calcium and other metals. These granules can then be stored or excreted; it is doubtful whether the heavy metals in these granules can exert a harmful action on the fish, but they may be transferred through the food chain to fish-eating animals. Similarly, chemicals such as DDT and PCBs that have a very low solubility in water but a high solubility in fat can be taken up from the water and the food chain and accumulate in fatty tissue. Again, the harm caused by these chemicals when they are in storage organs is uncertain, but it is thought that at times of food shortage the fat can be metabolized and the chemicals redistributed to other organs where they can cause damage.

It is unfortunate that most of the toxicity tests carried out with these accumulating elements and compounds have provided information only on the relationship between concentrations in the water and harmful effects on the fish. The relationship between concentrations in fish tissues and harmful effects is rarely studied and yet there is an increasing amount of information on the levels of these substances in fish and their predators because of their importance in the diet of man. In particular, attention has been focused on eels (MAFF 1989) because their high fat content allows them to accumulate a considerable amount of fat-soluble compounds;

these they take from the water, from the muddy sediments in which they live, and from their food, and they can be passed on to the people who eat them. But there is virtually no information on the effects of these accumulated levels on the fish themselves.

In practice, establishing this relationship between tissue concentration and fish health may be difficult. Methods of chemical analysis of fish tissues are designed to extract as much of the substance as possible, without distinguishing whether it was present at a site where it could cause damage or stored in a location where it was harmless. A similar problem exists with the analysis of sediments where it is difficult to differentiate between the amount of a substance that is available for uptake by organisms and that which is more firmly bound to the particles. It may be possible to predict the distribution of fat-soluble compounds between the various body tissues in the fish, but this may be valid only for the stage when equilibrium has been reached. A fish exposed to widely fluctuating concentrations of these compounds in the water and in the diet may not attain a state of internal equilibrium, particularly if the transfer pathways through the tissues for a substance entering via the gills (where it will be distributed through the arterial blood system) are different to the routes when it is absorbed by the gut and passed to the liver.

Clearly, these are difficult problems which must be borne in mind when designing experiments to measure the uptake and accumulation of chemicals by fish, and when making predictions based on the results obtained of the potential damage caused by the concentrations found in natural populations. At present, the main value of laboratory tests is to determine whether the potential for a fat-soluble chemical to accumulate in fish actually occurs in practice, or whether the substance can be metabolized, detoxified and excreted so that little or no accumulation takes place.

In the past, concern has been expressed that chemicals with a high potential for bioaccumulation might build up to high concentrations in organisms high up the food chain. For example, if a predator feeds on organisms with small amounts of such a chemical in their fatty tissues, the fat may be metabolized but the chemical will be retained and steadily accumulated in the fat deposits of the consumer. In practice, this does not occur to a significant extent in aquatic organisms although those animals with a high fat content such as eels may accumulate higher concentrations of these substances when expressed in terms of total body weight. However, birds and mammals that feed on fish and other aquatic life can accumulate high levels of these chemicals in their tissues; this is thought to be responsible in part for the decline in otter populations.

CONCLUSIONS

This chapter has given a brief overview of some of the many measurements that can be made on single fish, on populations and on communities in which fish are seen as part of a total ecosystem. An indication has been given of some of the complexities involved, not least in the interpretation of the data obtained. It has been said that when an experiment has been completed and the results worked out, the question that should then be asked is 'So what?'. There is a great temptation to read more into the results than is warranted, in order to emphasize their importance. Each experiment provides only a limited amount of factual information on which a certain amount of speculation and informed opinion can be based; it is important to keep these areas of fact and opinion separate. Indeed, it is equally important that the results themselves should be critically assessed by experts in order to ensure that they are well founded. Most scientific papers are reviewed by referees before they are published; however, the number of papers written increase each year and some which contain dubious results or conclusions can pass through the safety net (Lloyd 1986). The importance of reading a paper carefully when reviewing a certain subject area, and not relying on the abstract provided by the author, will become clear in Chapter 7 when water quality standards are discussed.

5 Effects of Some Common Pollutants on Fish

Although there are many thousands of chemicals which could find their way into water, only a few have occurred in sufficient concentrations to form a continuous threat to fish. These include zinc, copper, ammonia and suspended solids. But perhaps the greatest threat is that caused by the discharge of organic chemicals which can be rapidly oxidized by bacteria and so reduce the concentration of dissolved oxygen in the water. The examples of pollutants chosen in this chapter illustrate some of the complexities of the concentration-response relationships; further details on these and other common pollutants are given in reports produced by the Water Research Centre and the European Inland Fisheries Advisory Commission (EIFAC), listed in the References. The earlier EIFAC reports have been collated and updated by Alabaster & Lloyd (1982).

LOW DISSOLVED OXYGEN

Causes

Probably the most important cause of low levels of dissolved oxygen (DO) in rivers and lakes has been from the discharge of sewage effluents into waters where the dilution was insufficient to reduce the concentration of organic substances to acceptable levels. Improvement in the design and efficiency of sewage treatment plant has alleviated this ever-present problem to some extent. However, a number of other sources of organic discharges remain and these inputs are now assuming a greater importance. These include the accidental discharges of farm wastes from silage manufacture and from intensive livestock rearing, which contain very high concentrations of oxidizable organic matter. Also, strong organic wastes from food manufacture such as milk products and sugar refineries can be accidentally discharged directly to watercourses, or via sewage treatment works which may be unable to cope with the massive additional load. Losses of DO from the water can be replenished by re-aeration either through the surface, assisted by turbulence caused by riffles and waterfalls, or by the photosynthetic activity of plants during the daytime (it will be remembered from Chapter 3 that at night there will be a loss of oxygen from the water due to plant respiration). Therefore, the effect of a given 'biochemical oxygen demand' (BOD, expressed as the milligrams of oxygen used by bacteria to oxidize the organic matter in 1 litre (i.e. ppm) within a 5-day period) on the DO content of the water will vary according to the re-aeration rates at specific sites. In addition to the organic matter, ammonia (NH_3) present in these wastes (particularly those of animal origin) can be oxidized to nitrite (NO_2) and then to nitrate (NO_3) and so forms an additional oxygen demand.

Effect on fish respiration

The degree to which reducing the DO in the water raises the respiratory rate of fish, and thus increases the rate at which toxic chemicals can be taken up by the gills, was described in Chapter 3. But as DO levels fall the body metabolism will become affected by increasing suffocation, and very low levels will cause death. However, minor fluctuations in the DO content in water are a natural occurrence and so it is not surprising that fish have developed adaptive mechanisms to cope with these changes. When the DO of the water begins to fall, the fish increase the rate at which water is passed over the gills by increasing the rate and the depth of breathing. However, this reduces the respiratory efficiency of the gill lamellae, in part because the faster flow allows less time for the oxygen to be absorbed and in part because some water is forced past the tips of the gill filaments and therefore does not come into contact with the respiratory surfaces. This reduction in the mechanical efficiency of the gill is countered to some extent by an increase in the oxygen-carrying capacity of the blood. To achieve this, the blood volume is reduced and this is associated with an increase in urine flow; in this way the percentage volume of red blood corpuscles (haematocrit) is increased. This may then be followed by a release of extra blood corpuscles from stores in the spleen and kidneys and the return of the blood volume to normal. These effects, noted in rainbow trout, may take several hours to complete; other data suggest that full acclimation to a low DO may take up to 24 hours. Other processes such as a full utilization of the total gill respiratory surfaces may also occur. The general effect is that a respiratory system which is normally working well within its capacity is tightened up to perform at full efficiency. However, acclimation can compensate only for a moderate reduction in DO; for trout this may be down to 5 ppm compared with the normal value of, for example, 10 ppm at 15°C. At lower DOs the fish become increasingly stressed as the respiratory system becomes inadequate and unable to extract sufficient oxygen from the water to meet their basic metabolic needs. It is at this stage that fish may come to the water surface to gulp air in an attempt to increase the oxygen supply to the gills.

Limiting values

These general principles probably apply to all species of fish although much of the information has been obtained for species of salmon and trout. As these are active fish and normally live in cool, well-oxygenated waters, they are particularly sensitive to reductions in water DO. At the other end of the scale, species such as carp and goldfish which live in muddy ponds and warm, slow-flowing, rivers are much more resistant to low DO. It is difficult, therefore, to define a single limiting concentration of DO above which fish can flourish and below which they will be harmed. Much depends on the species of fish present, their DO requirements and their capacity for acclimation to low oxygen levels in the water.

There are two other factors that affect the ability of fish to withstand low DO. Because they are cold-blooded, their metabolism and therefore their oxygen requirements increase as the temperature rises. However, the solubility of oxygen in water decreases as the temperature increases; for example, at 5°C the solubility is 12.8 ppm and at 25°C it is 8.4 ppm. Therefore, a small drop in DO has a greater proportional effect in warm water than when it is cold. Also, the rate of bacterial decomposition of organic matter increases in warmer water, so low DO concentrations are more likely to occur under these conditions.

The second factor is that the bacterial decomposition of organic matter releases carbon dioxide into the water. This, too, affects the respiration of the fish because it reduces the rate at which the carbon dioxide produced by its own metabolism can diffuse from the blood into the water flowing over the gills. Indeed, high levels of carbon dioxide in the water can suffocate the fish by preventing the normal gas exchange at the gill surface from taking place, as well as affecting the amount of oxygen that can be taken up by the blood haemoglobin.

Fluctuating concentrations

The problem of low DO is therefore a complex one and it is difficult to examine the effects of all the various interactions by means of simple laboratory experiments. This is because the ideal experimental design is one in which a single factor only is varied, with the others being kept constant, so that any effects which are measured can be attributed quantitatively to that factor. Thus, fish have been exposed to a range of low

DO without prior acclimation and with normal levels of carbon dioxide in the water. The results obtained are difficult to extrapolate to natural conditions where the opposing factors of higher carbon dioxide levels and the acclimation by fish to the onset of low DO are also present. Also, the experimental DO is kept constant whereas in natural waters the concentrations may rise during the day and fall at night because of the photosynthetic activity of aquatic plants. The extent of these fluctuations will depend on other factors such as temperature and sunlight. Another factor will be the ability of fish in flowing waters to avoid areas of low DO; again, acclimation and also territorial behaviour may influence their behaviour in practice.

It is difficult, therefore, to take all these factors into account when assessing the effect of a continuous organic discharge on a fish population in the receiving water. This will be considered again in general in Chapter 7.

Fish kills

There remains the problem of sporadic discharges of strong organic wastes which can give rise to some devasting fish kills. These can occur during and after heavy rain which can overload sewers, or flush out stagnant ditches or slurry tanks associated with intensive agriculture. This gave rise in the past to the theory that fish could be killed by thunderstorms and indeed mortalities have been caused by lightning strikes. But the drop in DO following the discharge of organic matter can be very sudden and dramatic, and fish will be killed if the levels fall low enough and persist for a sufficient length of time. There is no time for acclimation and even avoidance action may be difficult if a sufficient length of river is affected by the discharge and the DO falls rapidly along the whole stretch. This situation is more akin to the conditions used in laboratory tests and factors such as higher concentrations of carbon dioxide which reduce survival times become increasingly important. This will be considered later when the effects of other mixtures of pollutants are examined. Although the short-term exposure of fish to low but sub-lethal levels of DO may increase their susceptibility to predation, especially if they are swimming at the surface or overturned, it is unlikely that their tissues will suffer long-term damage, and recovery will be complete on return to clean water. However, the position will be different if the water contains other chemicals in sufficient concentrations to be harmful when the respiration rate of the fish increases with the low DO.

Implications for monitoring

In summary, the discharge of biodegradable organic wastes to water imposes an additional complexity onto the existing natural fluctuating DO levels and on the physiological defences of the fish. In practice, the duration of exposure and the rate of acclimation of the fish are the critical factors in determining whether fish are harmed by low DO. Water quality standards cannot take all the relevant factors into account because of the complexity of the interactions and so the values set tend to be arbitrary and cautious (e.g. the standards set in the EEC Freshwater Fish Directive (1978) as given in Table 8.1, Chapter 8); it is quite possible to find good populations of fish in waters where a stringent or conservative standard is not met. Conversely, DO levels above the standard may still exacerbate the effects of harmful concentrations of toxic chemicals in the water.

AMMONIA

It is useful to consider ammonia at this stage because it is usually associated with organic wastes such as sewage effluents and slurry from intensive animal husbandry. Also, the complexity of the factors which are involved in affecting its toxicity to fish has something in common with those associated with low DO.

Chemistry in water

Ammonia exists in two forms in water – ionized NH_4^+ and non-ionized NH_3, sometimes referred to as un-ionized ammonia. The equilibrium between these two forms in water depends on the pH (acidity and alkalinity) and the temperature:

$$NH_4^+ + OH^- \rightleftharpoons NH_3 + H_2O$$

$\longrightarrow$

Increasing temperature

$\longrightarrow$

Increasing pH

Thus, an increase in pH from 7.0 to 7.3 will double the proportion of the non-ionized form in water containing ammonia. Similarly, an increase in temperature from 10°C to 20°C will have the same effect. This is very important, because it is the non-ionized form that is toxic to fish, and the ionized form has a very much lower toxicity that can be disregarded for all practical purposes. The actual concentration of ionized and non-ionized ammonia cannot be measured separately by chemical analysis; only the total ammonia present in the water can be measured. The proportion of the toxic non-ionized ammonia present is calculated by using equations that predict the ratio of the two forms present for a range of pH values and temperatures.

Therefore, even if the concentration of total ammonia remains constant in a natural water, variations in pH and temperature will change the amount of toxic non-ionized ammonia present. The pH of the water is largely controlled by the buffering action of bicarbonates + carbonates in relation to the carbon dioxide + carbonic acid equilibria, as shown below.

$$CO_2 + H_2O \rightarrow H_2CO_3 \rightarrow H^+ + HCO^-$$
carbonic anhydrase $\rightarrow$
$$CO_3^{2-} + H_2CO_3 \rightleftharpoons 2\ HCO_3^-$$

For a given amount of carbon dioxide in the water, the amount of carbonic acid and therefore the concentration of hydrogen ions (the pH) depends on the concentration of alkaline bicarbonate and carbonate ions present; the higher the latter, the more alkaline is the water. Conversely, for a given concentration of carbonate and bicarbonate ions in the water (the bicarbonate alkalinity), an increase in the concentration of carbon dioxide will increase the amount of acid hydrogen ions and so reduce the pH.

Effect of aquatic plants

Normally, the concentration of carbon dioxide in the water is in equilibrium with that in the air and is about 1.5 ppm. However, the photosynthetic and respiratory activities of plants (including algae) can make considerable changes to the amount present. During the day, plants remove carbon dioxide from the water during photosynthesis and in doing so they raise the pH of the water (Chapter 3). During the night, however, the dominant plant activity is respiration in which carbon dioxide is liberated into the water, thus reducing the pH. Unfortunately, it is difficult to obtain direct measurements of the amount of carbon dioxide in water, and these concentrations have to be calculated from equations which are based on the bicarbonate concentration, temperature and pH present (below pH 8, little carbonate is present and the alkalinity is due to bicarbonate). Therefore, during the summer when aquatic plants are growing vigorously, the water pH will rise during the day and fall at night. There will also be a general reduction in pH caused by the carbon dioxide produced by the oxidation of decaying organic matter, including that of plants at the end of the growing season. And finally, in those rivers where the flows vary considerably with the rainfall, the pH will fall after heavy rain because of the dilution of the bicarbonate content of the water.

Gill surface pH

All these factors that affect the pH of the water also affect the concentration of non-ionized ammonia present. But there is a further complication; the water in contact with the fish is that present at the gill surface, and the pH there is lowered by the respiratory carbon dioxide released from the blood. It was originally thought that this additional carbon dioxide would not affect the pH because the rate of the reaction to form carbonic acid was too slow in relation to the short residence time of the respiratory water in the gill chamber. However, recent research has shown that the enzyme carbonic anhydrase is present in the mucus covering the gill surface of rainbow trout (Wright *et al.* 1986), and presumably also of other species, and this catalyses the reaction so that it occurs very rapidly.

The extent to which the pH is changed at the gill surface depends on the amount of carbon dioxide produced by the fish, the concentration already present in the water, and the respiratory flow rate. Thus, under normal conditions the respiratory carbon dioxide could add an estimated extra 10 ppm to the water at the gill surface, although the exact amount will depend on the concentration of DO in the water and the efficiency of the extraction of this oxygen by the fish gills. If the DO of the water is reduced, then more water is passed over the gills to obtain the necessary oxygen and the carbon dioxide produced is correspondingly diluted by this additional flow. Therefore, it seems likely that a reduction in DO in the water will lead to a smaller reduction in pH at the gill surface of the fish.

The extent to which the pH is changed depends on the proportional increase in the concentration of carbon dioxide. Thus, a ten-fold increase from 1.0 to 10 ppm will cause a much greater reduction in pH than a two-fold increase from 10 to 20 ppm. It follows that the reduction in the toxicity of ammonia to fish caused by respiratory CO_2 will be greatest in water of low carbon dioxide content, because then the reduction in pH at the gill surface will be greater and therefore it will cause a correspondingly greater reduction in the proportion of ammonia present in the non-ionized form.

Obtaining direct experimental evidence of these predicted changes at the gill surface is almost impossible because the width of the channel between adjacent lamellae is very narrow and there is no pH measuring electrode that is small enough to be inserted into this space. However, the results of toxicity tests with ammonia tend to confirm predictions made with a model that incorporates all of the above factors.

If this model is correct, two important conclusions follow. The first is that ammonia will be much less toxic than predicted from the calculated concentration of the non-ionized form in water when the pH is high (greater than 8.0) because vigorous plant photosynthesis has removed much of the carbon dioxide there, and this has important implications for the application of water quality standards for ammonia under these conditions. The second relates to the conduct of laboratory toxicity test on the effect of ammonia on fish. A common practice has been to modify and control the pH of the experimental solutions by the addition of acid or alkali; the former can react with the bicarbonate in the water to increase the concentration of carbon dioxide present, and the latter reacts with carbon dioxide to reduce its concentration. Therefore, in tests designed to measure the effect of pH on the toxicity of ammonia, the results may be modified by differences in the concentration of carbon dioxide present; the general effect will be to make the solutions of lower pH more toxic than expected and the higher pH solutions less toxic.

It is unfortunate that the potential effect of respiratory carbon dioxide on the pH of the water at the gill surface was not recognized until recently in North America. The result is that much of the research carried out there in recent years on ammonia toxicity to fish is reduced in value because the concentrations of carbon dioxide in the test solutions were neither controlled nor measured. Some of these results purported to show that ionized ammonia exerted a low but measurable toxicity on fish in acid waters where the proportion of non-ionized ammonia present is very small. However, other data suggest that ionized ammonia concentrations of several hundred ppm would be required to cause mortality and such levels are most unlikely to occur in natural watercourses. The need for critical evaluations of these types of data before they are used to support water quality standards is emphasized in Chapter 7.

With so many variables affecting the ionization of ammonia in water, it is most unlikely that fish in natural waters will be exposed to steady concentrations of the toxic non-ionized fraction for any length of time. This has to be borne in mind when designing experiments to measure the toxicity of non-ionized ammonia to fish.

Toxicity to fish

Figure 5.1 shows the general shape of the toxicity curve obtained when fish are exposed to non-ionized ammonia. Concentrations above the threshold concentration are rapidly lethal, but with longer exposure a clearly defined threshold LC_{50} becomes apparent. Research has shown that this is probably caused by the rapid acclimation of the fish to elevated concentrations of ammonia in the water. This is not surprising because fish excrete their waste nitrogenous products formed by the breakdown of proteins mainly in the form of ammonia, and this excretion occurs mainly at the gill surface. Therefore,

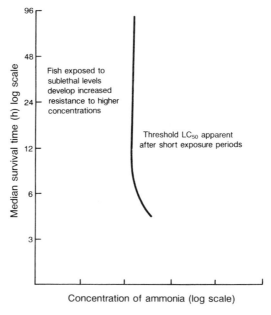

Fig. 5.1 Shape of the ammonia toxicity curve for rainbow trout.

an influx of non-ionized ammonia into the fish bloodstream might be countered by a build-up of the normal excretory mechanisms. It is known that fish which have been exposed to low, sub-lethal, concentrations of ammonia are more resistant to higher levels than are fish which have been kept in clean water. Indeed, fish kept under conditions of intensive farming where the excreted nitrogenous waste products can build up in the water appear to be more resistant than wild fish to non-ionized ammonia. It is possible, but not proven, that fish such as farmed trout which are fed on high protein pellets may have a more highly developed mechanism for ammonia excretion than those which have fed on a more meagre natural diet.

Ammonia excretion

The exact mechanism for ammonia excretion at the gill surface is uncertain; an authorative review of the processes involved has been made by Randall & Wright (1987). It was thought that excreted ionized ammonia was coupled with the active uptake of sodium from the water, but later studies suggested that the sodium was exchanged with hydrogen ions from the blood. Also, the chloride taken up by the fish is exchanged with bicarbonate from the blood, so in effect the salt uptake is balanced by the excretion of respiratory carbonic acid). It is possible, therefore, that the excretion of ammonia from the gills is achieved by the diffusion of non-ionized ammonia from the blood into the water; however, in this case the presence of higher non-ionized ammonia concentrations in the water would reduce or even halt the rate of excretion. This does not appear to occur, so in these circumstances ammonia may be actively exchanged for sodium in the water. Some evidence to support this possibility is that fish exposed to ammonia for several days showed progressive acidity of the blood which may have been due to the reduced excretion of hydrogen ions, but in other similar experiments no such reduction in blood pH was recorded.

Water balance

Another effect of ammonia toxicity is to increase the rate at which water enters the fish, as measured by the volume of urine produced. The increase in urine production occurs shortly after the fish are exposed to higher levels of ammonia in the water and in rainbow trout (the only species in which this effect has been measured) the flow rate increases six-fold as the 96 h LC_{50} is approached. In sub-lethal concentrations the flow rate was reduced after 24 h, suggesting that some acclimation was taking place. However, after a few days in clean water the fish appeared to lose their protective acclimation.

Species sensitivity

The resistance of fish to ammonia toxicity, therefore, depends in part on their immediate history of exposure to this chemical and perhaps in part on their diet. This introduces another set of factors into the sources of variability in experimental results. Many of the basic studies have been carried out with salmonid species, and less is known about the reactions of other fish. In general, there appears to be little difference in the sensitivity of different species to acutely lethal concentrations of ammonia, but longer term studies suggest that non-salmonid species, in particular the less active ones, are slightly more resistant to ammonia. Very little is known about the ability of these species to acclimate to ammonia in the water. Indeed, the metabolic cost of acclimation is not known for any species although a reduction in fish growth rate has been measured in some longer term experiments. This would suggest that some of the energy obtained from the food eaten by the fish was diverted to maintaining the additional excretion of ammonia from the gills, or repairing the harmful effects caused by an increased permeability of the gills to water; alternatively, the amount of food eaten may have been reduced.

Limiting concentrations

Clearly, there is much more to be learnt about the toxicity of ammonia to fish and it is important that more work should be carried out because of the widespread occurrence of this chemical both in natural waters as well as in intensive fish culture. The major factors known to affect ammonia toxicity are shown in Table 5.1; sufficient is known about these to enable a valid water quality standard for ammonia to be set for the protection of fish. The present standard in the EEC Directive (1978) for the protection of fish is 0.025 ppm as non-ionized NH_3 (Table 8.1, Chapter 8); this is set for the protection of all species of fish, so it may be slightly over-protective for some of the more resistant species. A slightly less stringent standard may be appropriate for slow-moving waters containing sluggish fish species, particularly where

Table 5.1 Summary of the major factors that can affect the toxicity of ammonia to fish.

Physico-chemical properties of the water	
Temperature	Controls the proportion of toxic non-ionized ammonia present
pH	Controls the proportion of toxic non-ionized ammonia present
Dissolved oxygen (DO)	Low DO increases ammonia toxicity
Effect of plants	
Photosynthesis	Increases DO
	Reduces CO_2 → increases pH of water
Respiration	Reduces DO
	Increases CO_2 → reduces pH of water
Effects at gill surface	
CO_2 excretion	Increased DO increases CO_2 excretion → reduces pH of water
	Increased CO_2 in incoming water lessens the extent to which pH is reduced
Acclimation	
Environmental NH_3	Increased detoxification capability? Linked with protein content of food?

the pH can rise above 8.0 and the toxicity of non-ionized ammonia is reduced. It should be noted that the water quality standard applies to the direct toxic action of ammonia on fish; a different standard is required to control the effect of ammonia on the trophic status of the water. High levels of ammonia will help to promote heavy weed and algal growth which can be detrimental to fish. Also, the oxidation of ammonia to nitrate by bacteria can cause a depletion of the dissolved oxygen in the water. For these reasons, there is a need to set a standard for the concentration of total ammonia in water.

Implications for monitoring

Finally, there remains the problem of proper water sampling to ensure that the standard is being met in a watercourse. The accurate calculation of the concentration of non-ionized ammonia in the water depends on reliable measurements of the pH and the total ammonia concentration; these measurements may be difficult if the pH is affected by unstable high or low levels of carbon dioxide in the water and the ammonia concentration is affected by bacterial oxidation of ammonia to nitrate in the sample bottle before analysis. Therefore, there will be a greater uncertainty about the accuracy of the calculated concentration than about that of other chemicals measured in the water. Also, the concentration of non-ionized ammonia obtained applies only to that point in time when the sample was taken; this problem is true, of course, for all spot samples and is normally overcome by taking frequent measurements so that the variability can be assessed. But a bias can be introduced if the night-time concentrations are different from those in the day; as described earlier, day-time pH values of natural waters can be higher than normal if the plant and algae are actively removing carbon dioxide for photosynthesis. Samples taken during the day will therefore contain higher concentrations of non-ionized ammonia than would be present at night, and might differ considerably from the true average 24 h value for that particular site.

The calculated effect of ammonia on fish populations would, then, appear to be worse than it was in practice. Also, no allowance is made in the standard for the ability of fish to acclimate to ammonia, and it may be possible for them to adapt to the daily rise and fall in concentration. Because of all these factors, it is quite possible that good fish populations will exist in waters where the sampling programme shows that the non-ionized ammonia standard is exceeded, because of analytical difficulties, sample bias and fish acclimation. Of these, sample bias can be overcome by automatic monitors which continuously measure pH, temperature and total ammonia. But even then, it is difficult to establish the relation between the fluctuating non-ionized ammonia levels found in natural waters and a standard based on laboratory data obtained with exposure of fish to constant concentrations. It is very difficult to make a proper assessment of the actual hazard to fish in such situations. In view of all these problems, the use of an overprotective standard may be justified as a precaution, but the position should be re-affirmed if adherence to this standard requires the construction of additional expensive treatment works.

HEAVY METALS

Historically, heavy metals (i.e. zinc, copper, lead, cadmium, etc.) rank as major polluting chemicals in both developed and developing countries.

Sources

Probably the most important heavy metal source was, and still is in some countries, the waste waters arising from mining activities, such as mine drainage water, effluent from tailings ponds (where waste crushed ore is settled out) and drainage water from spoil heaps. These sources can continue to discharge heavy metals into watercourses long after the original mining activities have ceased. This problem was recognized in the last century and formed one of the first topics for research on the effects of pollution on fish. In the UK this research centred around the rivers draining the mine workings in mid-Wales where even now the heavy metal inputs from abandoned sites continue to affect the fish life there.

Another important source is the industries that use these metals in various processes, especially electroplating and galvanizing of iron, where waste solutions from the treatment vats are discharged without treatment. Strict controls on these discharges are reducing the scale of this problem in developed countries. However, the widespread use of these metals in a variety of products and their slow corrosion and erosion leads to a general diffuse input into watercourses. For example, the use of galvanized iron and copper pipes in domestic water supplies contributes to elevated levels of zinc and copper in sewage effluents. Because these metals are elements, they cannot disappear from the environment; they can only be transferred from one place to another. Thus, although some of the metal will remain in solution, a proportion will be accumulated in the sediments, either in freshwater, estuaries or the sea. It is the build-up of these metals over many decades in sediment 'sinks' that is of major concern today, especially in the marine environment.

Although the heavy metals are often referred to as a common group of pollutants, the individual metals pose different problems in the freshwater environment and therefore they have to be considered separately.

Zinc

Because of the relatively high solubility of zinc compounds, this metal occurs widely in freshwaters. Indeed, it is important that it should do so because it is an essential element for aquatic life; for example, it occurs in the enzyme carbonic anhydrase which, as described previously, catalyses the formation of carbonic acid from carbon dioxide in the blood. Small amounts in the water or in the diet are therefore essential; it also follows that the organisms will have an internal mechanism to transport zinc around the body in order to manufacture such vital enzymes. When the zinc in the water rises to a level where the amount entering the organism through the gills exceeds the requirement for this metal, the surplus has to be excreted and this will require a certain amount of energy. At higher levels this detoxification mechanism may be insufficient to cope with the influx and the zinc will then exert a direct toxic action.

Toxic effects of zinc

It was originally thought that the direct toxic action of zinc on fish was to precipitate the layer of mucus on the surface of the gills, causing suffocation. While this may still be true for those species which produce a copious supply of mucus, the white precipitate observed on the gills of, say, rainbow trout is mainly composed of disintegrating epithelial cells which may be associated with the onset of mortality. However, zinc may also cause a certain amount of tissue damage by reacting with proteins and this could effect the respiratory efficiency as well as the osmoregulatory function of the gills.

The major environmental factor which affects the toxicity of zinc to fish is the calcium concentration of the water. Calcium, like zinc, is a divalent ion and both compete for binding sites on protein molecules. Although some competition may occur on the gill surface, the main site of action may be inside the epithelial cell where the calcium concentration is in equilibrium with that in the surrounding water. Therefore, if fish are removed from a hard, calcium-rich, water to a soft water, they will slowly lose their resistance to zinc toxicity as their body calcium is reduced to a lower equilibrium level. The relationship between the concentration of zinc acutely toxic to rainbow trout and the hardness of the water is shown in Fig. 5.2. Similar data exist for other species of fish, although in some cases an inadequate acclimation period to different water hardnesses may affect the extent of the differences obtained.

As might be expected, sub-lethal concentrations of zinc

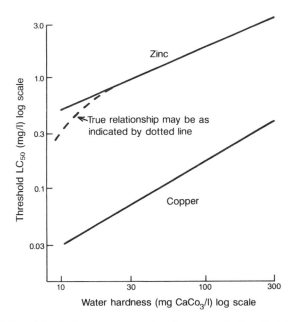

Fig. 5.2 Relationship between water hardness and threshold LC_{50}s for rainbow trout exposed to zinc and copper solutions.

have been shown to reduce the growth rate and the fecundity of various fish species, but whether this is due to a reduced food intake or the increased energy expenditure on tissue repair and detoxification processes is unclear. It is possible that there is an irritant effect on the gill epithelium because it has been observed that there is an increased frequency of coughing; this may be the reason for the observed avoidance reaction by fish to zinc contaminated waters.

In general, these sub-lethal effects occur at concentrations down to one-tenth of the threshold LC_{50}; at lower concentrations the normal physiological processes that control the required level of zinc in the body are probably sufficient to cope with the extra influx. There is some evidence that fish can become acclimatized to higher levels of zinc in the water, partly because of an enhanced detoxification capacity. For example, brown trout are found in the R. Ystwyth in Wales where the zinc levels are close to those that would be toxic to unacclimatized fish. However, these fish may be unable to breed successfully in such waters because of the sensitivity of their early life stages to this metal.

Implications for monitoring

In those rivers which drain old mining areas the levels of zinc will fluctuate considerably with the rainfall; the onset of heavy rain may produce a peak concentration from the flushing out of stagnant water in the spoil heaps, and this will be followed by a rapid decline with the increased dilution by run-off from the surrounding area. Such peak concentrations seem to be better withstood by older, larger fish for these short periods than by the more sensitive fry. The main problem is accounting for these fluctuations when assessing whether the river complies with the water quality standard set to protect fish. The sampling programme may not coincide with the sporadic peaks of high zinc concentration, and on the rare occasions when a peak is recorded its duration will not be measured so that its implication for the fish population remains unknown.

In other waters where the zinc inputs are derived from more stable sources the fluctuations will be less marked and the normal sampling programme will be adequate to describe the levels to which the fish are exposed. The standards set for zinc in the EEC Freshwater Fish Directive (1978) take into account the effects of water hardness (Table 8.1), but in soft waters the hardness may vary considerably with the rainfall and so it may be difficult to define an appropriate standard.

Copper

The main sources of copper are similar to those of zinc, with mining activities producing important point sources of pollution and a more general diffuse input from the use of the metal for water pipes and other purposes. In some respects the toxicity of copper to fish is also similar to that of zinc; indeed, it is also an essential trace element but it has also been widely used at high concentrations as a very effective algicide and molluscicide. It is not surprising that copper is potentially more toxic to fish than zinc.

Toxic effects of copper

Good experimental data on copper toxicity are more difficult to obtain than for zinc. In hard water, copper precipitates out as a basic carbonate which is very slow to redissolve. It is difficult to prepare experimental solutions in such waters because the colloidal precipitate which can be formed is not acutely toxic and the amount of copper present in the toxic ionized form may be variable. Also, soft waters can often contain dissolved organic material such as humic acids derived from peat, and these can form complexes with copper. These cupro-organic complexes have a much lower toxicity than the free ionized metal. Analyses of copper in water measure the concentration of total metal present and they do not normally distinguish between the toxic soluble form and the less toxic colloidal and organically complexed forms.

In some fish toxicity tests where the solutions were not renewed frequently, the organic matter produced by the fish might be able to complex some of the copper. The solution would then be rendered less toxic, thus producing higher LC_{50}s than would be otherwise obtained if all the copper was present in an ionic form. Also, copper sulphate has been widely used in the past as an algicide in fish-bearing waters, at concentrations which would be toxic if the metal was present in the toxic ionized form. In practice, no fish mortalities have been reported as a result of these operations, presumably because the copper was rapidly precipitated or complexed into much less toxic forms. However most, if not all, of this inactive copper will ultimately enter sediment sinks where it may have a limited bioavailability for organisms living there. Again, this is an area where more research is required.

The acute toxic action of copper seems to be similar to that of zinc; also, there are similar reports of sub-lethal effects occurring at concentrations down to 10% of the threshold LC_{50}. For example, growth rates of fish are affected at these concentrations and for copper this may be due to a reduced rate of feeding or an increased rate of activity. However, there is little laboratory or field evidence for acclimation by fish to low levels of copper in the water. To some extent this is due to the problems in determining the actual amount of toxic copper present.

As with zinc, the main environmental factor affecting the toxicity of copper is the calcium concentration of the water (Fig. 5.2), again because of the competition between these two ions for binding sites in the tissues of the gills and other organs. However, in contrast to zinc, salmonid species are not the most susceptible to copper toxicity; for example, perch may be three times as sensititive as rainbow trout to this metal. The reason for this difference in species sensitivity is not known and it is possible that the toxic actions of copper and zinc are in some way slightly different. The EEC Freshwater Fish Directive (1978) sets standards for copper that are common to both salmonid and cyprinid species, but takes into account the effect of water hardness and allows for the formation of less toxic organo-copper complexes (Table 8.1, Chapter 8).

Lead

Although lead has a high profile in human toxicology, it is of much lesser importance for aquatic life. This is mainly due to a low solubility which limits its occurrence at significant concentrations in all but very soft waters. Sub-lethal effects include the darkening of the tails of salmonid fish and this can be diagnostic of low levels of lead in the water. Some evidence of this effect has been found in fish from rivers receiving discharges from old lead mines in mid-Wales. Calcium may have a modifying effect on the toxicity of lead to fish, but this will be significant only in soft acid waters where toxic concentrations can occur. Diffuse inputs of lead into surface waters arising from its widespread use in petrol and batteries may increase the concentrations in sediments but this does not appear to be significant for aquatic life.

Cadmium

Again, this metal has a high profile in human toxicology because of cases where it has been transferred at harmful concentrations to man through the food chain. In water, the main point source is effluents from electroplating works; also, there are numerous diffuse inputs from the widespread use of this metal as well as a few areas where cadmium is leached from geological deposits. Cadmium is strongly adsorbed onto organic and inorganic particles in the water but, although it can form soluble complexes with humic substances, the toxicity is not reduced as it is with copper, at least not in hard water. However, it is the binding on to solid particles that limits the importance of total cadmium levels in the water, but again most, if not all, of the bound metal will end up in sediment sinks. There is some evidence that this cadmium is available, to a limited extent, to invertebrates living in the sediment and can be passed on to fish which prey on them (Douben 1989). However, the potential for significant accumulation by this route is uncertain and requires further research.

Toxic effects of cadmium

Calcium appears to reduce the toxicity of soluble toxic concentrations of cadmium in the water, but to a lesser extent than that for zinc and copper. There is, however, a major difference between cadmium's toxic action and that of the other heavy metals, in that there appear to be two separate and successive harmful effects. For rainbow trout, the toxicity curve over the first four days follows the normal shape for heavy metals and appears to approach a threshold value. However, continuation of the exposure causes mortalities at much lower concentrations and a further threshold is reached at a concentration considerably less than the 96 h LC_{50}. The most logical explanation is that the efficiency of the detoxification mechanism for cadmium in the fish has a limited duration and therefore acts as only a short-term brake on the internal toxic action.

Because the efficiency of this defensive mechanism can

vary with the life stage of the fish, and between different species of fish, the use of data on the short-term toxicity of cadmium for comparative purposes can be misleading, depending on whether or not this secondary effect occurs, or begins to occur, within the period of the test. This is a good example of the errors which can occur if too much reliance is placed on a 96 h LC_{50} value as a measure of toxicity for defining comparative effects of different variables. It is essential for this purpose that the shape of the toxicity curve should be established for prolonged periods of exposure. It is possible that much of the variation in the susceptibility of fish to cadmium concentrations in the range 0.01−1.0 mg/l is due to the variability in the efficiency of the defence mechanism.

Other heavy metals

There is much less information on the toxicity to fish of other heavy metals such as nickel, chromium and vanadium, mainly because of their lower importance as actual pollutants in the freshwater environment. Comprehensive reviews of the published data are available and the information should be assessed in the light of the comments which have already been made on potential sources of error. A reference should be made here to the toxicity of mercury which also had a high profile in recent decades because of its transfer to man by fish in the diet. Mercury can be taken up by fish as the inorganic form but the main route is by absorption of mercury which has been methylated by bacterial action in sediments. However, the standards set for safe levels of mercury in fish for human consumption are lower than those that affect fish, so the importance of this metal to fish populations is much reduced if the public health standards are met.

This raises a point that was made in Chapter 4: an increasing amount of data is being accumulated on the levels of heavy metals in fish as part of general environmental monitoring programmes, yet much of the information on effects on fish is related to levels of these elements in water and not in the edible tissues. It is difficult, if not impossible, to use these data on tissue concentrations to predict the consequences for the health of the fish. This is a serious gap in our knowledge because the levels in fish reflect the variations in the exposure concentrations, their bioavailability, and the sum of different routes of uptake. It is true that the correlations may not be simple because the form of the metal in the fish (in granules or attached to proteins) may not be revealed by chemical analysis, but it is clear that there is a need for better collaboration between the ecotoxicologists and the chemists to fill this gap in the same way as has occurred, to a limited extent, with some of the pesticides.

ACID RAIN

Acid rain has a high profile in the public's perception of atmospheric pollution, but for freshwaters it is not the pH of the rain that is important but the acidity of the run-off water.

Causes of surface water acidity

The main cause of the acidification of upland streams is the deposition of sulphur and nitrogen oxides from the atmosphere via rainfall onto soil overlying a granite substratum. These oxides can be converted to sulphuric and nitric acids which can then be transferred by leaching and run-off into watercourses. Where the substratum is not granite but other types of rock, the acids may be neutralized by the natural alkaline salts that they contain. Granite contains very little alkaline salts which is why the streams arising in such catchment areas are naturally on the acid side of neutrality. Therefore, although the acidity of the rain falling on land in the eastern areas of England, for example, is greater than that falling on the granite areas in the north-west, it is the streams in the latter area that have become acidified.

The detailed mechanisms of all the various interactions involved are extremely complex and in many cases poorly understood. It must be remembered that acid flushes in moorland streams can be a natural event; for example, heavy rain after a period of drought will wash out peat bogs that have become very acid in the dry weather, and there are recorded instances where this has caused the deaths of many fish. Changes in land use and agricultural practices also affect the neutralizing capacity of the soil. The planting of conifers on poor soil leads to an increase in acidification, whereas the liming of upland pastures to improve the production of grass in sheep pastures may have had an ameliorating effect. Indeed, the liming of catchment areas is now a recognized method of reducing the acidity of catchments where the deposition of acid salts has become a problem. The biological activity of the different types of vegetation in the catchment area may also be a factor in affecting the acidity of the run-off water.

Toxicity to fish

As the pH of the water falls below 5.5, so the harmful effects on fish begin to increase. These can be direct harmful effects on the ability of the fish to maintain their natural salt balance, especially in water with a very low calcium content, or indirect effects such as that from a reduced food supply. There is a reduction in the productivity of natural waters at these low pH values because the recycling of nutrients is inhibited. Sudden increases in acidity to pH values below 4.5 may be lethal to fish; in general, the salmonid species are more resistant than other families of fish because they are adapted to living in acid waters.

Importance of aluminium

Surveys of the fish populations in acid waters indicated that in many cases there were apparent harmful effects at pH levels that would be considered acceptable on the basis of laboratory experiments. The cause of this extra toxicity was found to arise from the leaching of heavy metals by the acids from the underlying rock and, more recently, attention has focused on aluminium as the most important element. A comprehensive review of the chemistry of aluminium and its effects on fish and other aquatic organisms has been published by Howells *et al.* (1990).

The toxicity of aluminium to fish is extremely complex because it can exist in many different chemical forms in water, depending on the pH, and these forms have differing toxicities. The most toxic chemical form is found within the pH range 5.2−5.8, and this may account for the reduced populations of fish found in waters with this range of acidity. As with other metals, the toxicity of aluminium is reduced when the calcium concentration of the water is increased, and added protection is also given by silicon salts.

The correlation between the results of laboratory experiments and field observations on the effects of low pH and aluminium is made difficult because of the problems of controlling the acidity of test solutions to the required accuracy in the former, and the wide seasonal fluctuations in the latter which can depend on the frequency and extent of the rainfall or, in some cases, the snow melt. It should be pointed out that these fluctuations in chemical conditions are more severe in watercourses than in lakes where such changes are buffered by the large volume of water. However, there can still be effects on lake fish populations because the feeder streams where they may breed can be subject to intermittent harmful pulses of acidity.

The biological activities of the different types of vegetation in the catchment area may also be a factor in affecting the acidity of the run-off water. It is for these reasons that the effect of 'acid rain' on fisheries is still difficult to quantify, even though the main contributing factors to the problem have been identified and in some cases the concentration-effect relationships have been accurately established. But the example of acidity serves to illustrate the difficulties in establishing the harmful effects of diffuse inputs of chemicals, in this case from the atmosphere via the soil, on fisheries.

PESTICIDES

These chemicals are important as a potential hazard to aquatic life because they are designed and used to kill living organisms. It is beyond the scope of this book to describe in detail the effects of all the pesticides in common use; instead, a few examples will be given to indicate the types of problem encountered.

Organochlorine compounds

Historically, it was the persistant organochlorine pesticides (DDT, dieldrin, etc.) that formed the first focus of attention, mainly because they were very persistent in the environment and so were found far from the sites where they had been used to control local pests. These chemicals have been used not only in agriculture but also to control the insect vectors of disease; this use is continuing in developing countries where the problems of insect pests and insect-transmitted disease are severe and alternative methods of control are too expensive or insufficiently developed. These pesticides were also used by industry, for example in the moth-proofing of carpets where the effluents from the treatment processes were discharged to rivers. The recognition of the global distribution of these chemicals, aided by the increasing sensitivity of chemical analysis, has led to the steady withdrawal of their permitted uses as less persistent and effective alternative pesticides were developed.

Nevertheless, these chemicals remain in sinks, either terrestrial such as in land that has received repeated applications (e.g. dieldrin on narcissus fields and in soakaways from sheep dips) or in aquatic sediments. From there they will steadily diffuse and disperse into the wider environment.

Except where the usage of these chemicals was very high, or in watercourses receiving effluents that contained high concentrations, the damage caused to fisheries was probably very small. One reason for this is that these chemicals of low solubility bind strongly on to sediments and suspended particulate matter, so that the concentrations that occur in solution are extremely small.

However, it is possible that eels, which can accumulate high amounts of these chemicals in their fatty tissues, may be affected when they reach their breeding grounds in the Sargasso Sea. The mobilization of their fat reserves during the migration may release the stored pesticide so that it can affect other, more sensitive, tissues. Alternatively, the pesticide may be passed into the fat reserves of the eggs and so affect the developing larvae. Because so little is known about this stage of the eel's life history, it is difficult to prove whether these speculations are correct. As pointed out earlier, the main concern has been the transfer of sub-lethal levels of these pesticides through the food chain to fish-eating predators such as herons, birds of prey and otters.

Control of pesticides

The problems caused by these organochlorine compounds have led to increasingly strict controls being placed on the marketing and use of all pesticides. As a result, the possibility that the authorized use of these substances will cause damage to fisheries is becoming increasingly remote. There is always the possibility of water being polluted by accidental spillages or by the careless disposal of surplus spray and partially emptied containers. However, users of these chemicals are becoming increasingly aware of the potential dangers, so the incidence of such events should decrease. All pesticide containers should contain information on the potential harmfulness of the product to fish and other aquatic life, and the need to dispose of the contents safely.

It is possible that in the past, sporadic fish kills were

attributed to pesticides which were known to have been used locally, and because no other possible cause of the mortality was apparent. Records of the causes of freshwater pollution incidents in the UK arising from agriculture show that, in recent years, less than 2% are attributable to pesticides, compared with about 70% caused by the discharge of strong organic wastes. Even if some agricultural pesticide incidents go unreported, this statistic does put the importance of these compounds into perspective. However, in recent years there has been an increase in the number of incidents arising from the use or spillage of wood preservatives and controls on these products are being strengthened.

Obviously, pesticides which are to be used in or near water are given special attention, usually with comprehensive field experiments and trials, before approval for their use is given. This applies particularly to aquatic herbicides which, although they may have a low toxicity to fish, could cause secondary effects by the removal of plants which act as a necessary habitat for juvenile life-stages. For example, an early problem encountered with the use of paraquat was the rapid decay of the dead plants, causing a serious depletion in the DO of the water. Similarly, considerable caution is used for the approval of insecticides to control mosquitos in shallow standing waters, so as to ensure that fishery resources in the area are not affected. These are simple, clear-cut examples of the deliberate application of pesticides to water and where, if care is taken, the fisheries will remain unharmed.

There are less obvious and less direct examples; spray drift from pesticide application by land vehicles is unlikely to cause a problem in adjacent waters unless the product is extremely toxic and there is a strong wind. However, strict controls are applied to limit the climatic conditions under which pesticides can be applied. Similarly, stringent controls have to be applied to aerial applications to ensure that waterbodies are not oversprayed; this is more important when forests are sprayed to control insect pests because it is difficult to avoid overspraying small streams below the tree canopy.

Recent case histories

Tributyl tin
A different type of problem to that of organochlorine pesticides has been the use of tributyl tin (TBT) in antifouling paints for boats (Abel *et al.* 1987). These paints are designed to prevent aquatic life from settling on the underwater surface of the boat, usually by the incorporation of a pesticide in the formulation. Until recently, such paints were not included in the regulations that control pesticide use. Traditionally, the pesticide used in these formulations has been copper which, as described previously, is an algicide and also toxic in low concentrations to other aquatic life. However, the copper leaching from the paint surface is rapidly complexed with organic matter so that the immediate hazard is small; there is the longer-term problem of accumulation in sediment sinks. Within the last 15 years, the copper has been supplemented and then replaced by TBT, which does not form non-toxic complexes with organic material when leached but remains in a toxic form which slowly degrades to form less harmful compounds.

Although the problems of TBT have been more marked in the marine environment, high concentrations have been measured in freshwater areas where there is considerable boating activity, especially in marinas (Waite *et al.* 1989). Although the levels of TBT may not have been sufficiently high to have a direct effect on fish, it is possible that more sensitive organisms have been affected and led to secondary effects on fisheries. As a result of extensive research the use of organotin compounds in antifouling paints has now been prohibited by an EC Directive. Future developments in the use of toxic paints for boats in freshwaters must be carefully controlled.

Tecnazene on potatoes
Problems can arise with the change in the processing of agricultural products which have been treated with a pesticide. A recent example is the use of tecnazene to control fungal

infection and prevent early sprouting in stored potatoes (Whale *et al.* 1988). When the product was first approved for this use, the chance that it would get into watercourses seemed to be remote; any pesticide removed from the potatoes when they were prepared for cooking would be considerably diluted by domestic waste water and then treated by the normal sewage treatment processes. However, in recent years there has been an increasing demand for washed potatoes which are packed in transparent bags for sale. This has led to the proliferation of vegetable washing operations ranging from cottage industries to large installations. The effluent from many of these operations is discharged after some settlement directly to water, and so the tecnazene from the potato skin has a direct point source entry into the aquatic environment. Surveys have shown that in some cases the concentration of tecnazene in small streams receiving these effluents is sufficiently high to have a direct effect on fish if sustained for a few weeks. Investigations to determine the extent of this problem are continuing. An interesting side-issue is that the analytical technique commonly used to measure pesticide concentrations in water does not separate tecnazene from lindane, another common organochlorine pesticide, and so its occurrence in water may have gone unsuspected for several years; also, the concentrations reported for lindane in water may have been erroneously high if tecnazene was also present.

Implication for pesticide controls

It is difficult to forecast such events at the time of product registration and considerable time and effort is required to investigate such problems when they arise in order to establish a causal relationship with an observed effect, or establishing whether the concentrations occurring in water are having a significant effect on fish populations. However, the number of such problems are few in relation to the number of pesticides in use, and it is clear that the data submitted on the fate and effects of new products at the time of registration are sufficient for making an accurate prediction of the likely risk to aquatic life which would arise from their use. The data requirements for pesticide registration are steadily updated to take new information into account; at present the emphasis is on the rate at which pesticides leach from soil into the surface and underground water, either in solution or attached to soil particles.

CONCLUSIONS

The examples of pollutants given in this chapter were chosen not only because they are known to be important for fisheries but also because they illustrate the wide range of problems which can be encountered with different types of chemicals. It is clear that there are complex inter-relationships between the concentration of a pollutant in the water and its effect on fish. These have to be quantified in order to assess whether the concentration of a pollutant is having an effect on fish populations, and for setting appropriate water quality standards.

In particular, the descriptions given above highlight the two major problems associated with establishing the relationship between the presence of a toxic chemical in water and its effect on fish:

(1) Accidental spillages. These can lead to high concentrations in the water and the effects on fish will be associated with acute toxicity. In these circumstances the duration of exposure may be critical, but such events are most unlikely to be picked up by routine monitoring programmes. Therefore, there will not be a quantitative chemical description of the event available which can then be compared with laboratory data on concentration − effect relationships.

(2) Concentrations of chemicals derived from continuous discharges of effluents to watercourses. These are unlikely to remain constant and the fluctuations may allow for a

variable degree of acclimation by the fish present. However, laboratory data are invariably derived from experiments in which the fish are continuously exposed to the chemical, so that they do not reflect natural conditions.

The implications of these two problems in the context of pollution control will be considered in Chapter 7.

6 Toxicity of Mixtures

The previous chapter provided a brief overview of the relationships between common pollutants and fish, and the effect of various natural water characteristics on them. These pollutants were considered singly, but in practice a water body is more likely to contain a number of different pollutants at the same time. This has given rise to fears that such mixtures may be much more toxic than expected, and references have been made to 'cocktails' of chemicals which imply that the end effect will be greater than the sum of the individual components. There have been very few reviews of the effects of mixed pollutants on fish and other aquatic life; a review by EIFAC was prepared in 1980 and an updated version is in Alabaster & Lloyd (1982). A further updating was carried out (EIFAC 1987) and a modified version published by Alabaster *et al.* (1988). A wider review on the effects of mixtures on organisms in general is given in Vouk *et al.* (1987).

DEFINITIONS

It is important at the outset to define the use of the term 'mixture'. In this chapter, the toxicity of mixtures refers to the combined effects of two or more chemicals on the fish; it does not refer to any effects which arise from a reaction between these chemicals in the water. For example, the raising of the pH of the water from 6.5 to 8.0 by the addition of an alkali such as caustic soda will of itself not affect fish, but it will increase considerably the toxic proportion of non-ionized ammonia present. This increased toxicity is caused by a chemical reaction occurring in the water and is not appropriate in a description of the toxicity of mixtures to fish.

There is a range of effects that can occur when fish are exposed to two or more chemicals in the water. At one end of the scale the joint action can be 'synergistic' if the effects are much greater than would be expected from the known toxicities of the individual chemicals. If there is only a slight increase in toxicity, the joint action is described as 'more than additive'. 'Additive' joint action occurs when the effect is the sum of the known toxicities of the individual chemicals. Below this comes 'less than additive' and 'no addition', which are self-explanatory. Finally, there is 'antagonism', where the toxicity of one or more of the chemicals in the mixture is significantly reduced. The type of joint action that occurs in a mixture will depend on the toxic action of the individual chemicals.

RELATIONSHIP TO TOXIC ACTION

All chemicals, if present in a sufficiently high concentration, have the same toxic action on fish in that they will cause a blockage in the cell membranes and so prevent the transfer of essential chemicals through them. This type of blockage is referred to as a physical effect because it does not involve any chemical reactions with normal physiological processes. Such an action leads to narcosis or anaesthesia, because the normal processes of ion transfer in and out of the cells of the nervous system are blocked. One of the best known examples is that of alcohol, which has the same type of effect on fish as it does on man.

However, many chemicals react with and affect the physiological processes within the body at much lower concentrations than those producing a physical effect, and these are known as chemical effects. It is obvious that there can be a wide variety of chemical reactions that can be affected in the body; indeed, the development of selective pesticides depends on finding a chemical that reacts with a process within the target species at a concentration lower than that which affects other processes in non-target organisms. Other substances that exert a chemical effect on a physiological process which is present in a wide range of organisms are not suitable as selective pesticides.

Therefore, at one end of the scale of toxic actions there might be placed a selective pesticide that has a unique effect on no more than a few species at a low concentration, while the other end will contain a group consisting of a large number of substances that have no chemical effect but produce narcosis by a physical blocking of the cell membranes. In between these two extremes will be a range of substances which can be divided into separate groups, according to the type of chemical effect that they exert on organisms.

MEASUREMENT OF COMBINED ACTION

There are two ways whereby the joint toxic action of these chemicals can be measured. The first is known as 'concentration addition' in which the concentrations required to produce a given response, such as a threshold LC_{50}, are used in the calculations. This method is important in the context of water quality standards because the permitted concentrations may have to be modified when there are several potentially harmful chemicals in the water. The second is 'response addition' in which the joint action of chemicals on the survival time of the organism is measured. This approach has been widely used in pesticide research where there is a requirement for mixtures that kill the target organism (usually insects) in the shortest possible time. In terms of fisheries protection this approach is relevant in assessing the impact of short-term spills, when a potential reduction in survival time caused by a mixture of chemicals will be important because it will increase the area within which fish are harmed.

TOXICITY OF SIMPLE MIXTURES

Investigations on the toxicity of mixtures to fish have usually been made with short-term tests in which the toxicity curves are obtained for the single chemicals and these are compared with the curve for the mixture in which the subtances are usually present in equitoxic proportions. It is essential that the threshold LC_{50}s are used as a measure of the definitive response because these represent an equilibrium condition between the fish and the concentration of chemical in the water and are therefore a true measure of the sensitivity of the fish. If, as a result of such an experiment, it is found that the threshold LC_{50} for chemical A is 10 mg/l and for chemical B 2 mg/l, and that the threshold value for a mixture of the two is obtained when the concentration of A is 5 mg/l and B is 1 mg/l, then the combined action is called additive, because half a toxic concentration of A plus half a toxic concentration of B produces a threshold LC_{50}. This becomes easier to understand if the threshold LC_{50} for a given chemical and species of fish is given a value of 1 Toxic Unit (TU). In the example given above, the mixture contained 0.5 TU of chemical A and 0.5 TU of chemical B; the combined toxicity was 1.0 TU, which was a threshold LC_{50}.

Physical toxic action

Considerable research has shown that those chemicals which have a primarily physical toxicity are additive at all concentrations; for example, it has been shown that a mixture of 50 organic chemicals, each at one-fiftieth of their individual threshold concentration (0.02 TU), acted in a strictly additive manner and produced a toxic solution. It should be stressed that it is the fractions of the threshold LC_{50}s that are additive, not the actual concentrations. The mechanism behind this additive action will be described in Chapter 7.

Chemical toxic action

The situation is not so simple for substances that have a chemical effect on fish, and the following is a simplified summary of present knowledge. As such, it contains broad generalizations to which there are certain to be exceptions. At sufficiently high concentrations, all these substances have a common effect in that they cause mortality. Therefore, concentrations that are close to the threshold LC_{50} (e.g. >0.3 TU), are additive when present in a mixture. At lower concentrations, only those that have identical toxic actions will be additive; those with different toxic actions will show a decreasing additivity, and at levels at which the individual chemicals have no significant effect (when the detoxification mechanisms can fully cope with the amount of chemical entering the body) they have no additive action. It has been pointed out that one way of determining whether two substances have a common toxic action is to find out if they act in an additive manner in a mixture. If this is to be measured by short-term toxicity tests, then one of the chemicals will need to be present at <0.2 TU, to avoid the general additive effect that occurs at higher concentrations. There is a problem here in that fish toxicity tests are not sufficiently accurate to measure the small increase in toxicity which would be contributed by a chemical at, say, 20% of the threshold LC_{50} (0.2 TU). However, the principle seems to be correct and requires further research to establish its validity.

If fish toxicity tests are carried out with two chemicals, A and B, their individual toxicity curves may take the shape of those shown in Fig. 6.1. In this graph, the concentrations are expressed as TUs to make the comparison between the curves easier. For many mixtures tested, the toxicity curve will be positioned between those for the individual chemicals when the concentrations of A and B, expressed as TUs, are similar. If the ratio of chemical A to chemical B (expressed as TUs) was 3:1, that is, A contributed three times as much toxicity to the mixture as B, then the shape of the toxicity curve would be closer to that obtained for chemical A. As the concentration

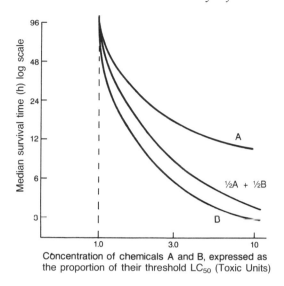

Fig. 6.1 Diagrammatic toxicity curves for fish exposed to two chemicals (A and B), singly, and as an equitoxic mixture.

of chemical B is reduced further, so it is less likely that it will act in an additive manner with chemical A, if their toxic actions are dissimilar.

Most of the toxicity tests with mixtures of chemicals with dissimilar toxic action have been carried out with two or three compounds and these indicate that in the majority of cases the combined toxicity is either additive or less than additive. This is the case even with pesticides with dissimilar toxic action that are applied in practice as mixtures (Matthiessen *et al.* 1988).

Where more substances were included in the mixture, then the combined toxicity becomes increasingly less than additive. This can be explained by the fact that in these multiple mixtures the individual concentrations become closer to the level that causes no harmful effect. In theory, a mixture of 10 chemicals, each at a concentration of 0.1 TU, would not be toxic if these concentrations were not additive in their combined action, even though the sum of the TUs was 1.0. However, if the mixture was three times more concentrated so that the individual chemicals were at 0.3 TU, and if these concentrations were then additive in their toxic action, the combined concentration of 3.0 TU would be highly toxic. This hypothesis has not been tested, but it would be important in the context of complex effluents where the toxicity may be reduced after discharge at a rate greater than would be expected from the rate of dilution, because the combined toxicities of the components will become increasingly less than additive.

Reduction in survival time

Because this description of combined action has so far focused on concentrations close to and below the threshold LC_{50}s, the conclusions are relevant to the setting of quality standards for fish in waters containing a number of chemicals that have the potential to cause pollution. In this context, there is no evidence that mixtures of these chemicals can have a more than additive combined action; there is no evidence for synergism and the fear of a 'cocktail' effect is without scientific foundation. However, there are a few cases of a more than additive effect occurring in lethal mixtures. For example, Fig. 6.2 shows the result of a fish toxicity test with copper and zinc. The shapes of the individual toxicity curves are identical, suggesting that the two metals have a common or very similar toxic action, but at lethal concentrations the survival times of the fish in the mixture are much shorter than those fish exposed to the individual metals. This suggests that a synergistic action in terms of response addition occurs at these high concentrations. This could be important for two reasons:

(1) It implies that an accidental spillage or high discharge of these two metals could harm a fish population in a shorter period of time than would be expected from the survival times for exposure to the individual metals; that is, sudden high concentrations will be more harmful than expected.

(2) The pattern of effects described in (1) above may occur for chemicals whose toxicity curves for fish do not attain

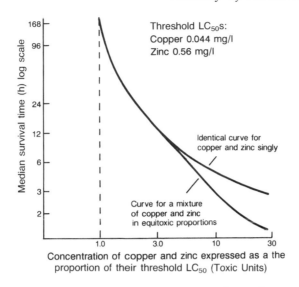

Fig. 6.2 Toxicity curves for rainbow trout exposed to solutions of copper and zinc, singly and as a mixture, in soft water (redrawn from Lloyd 1961).

a threshold LC_{50} until several weeks of exposure, in which case an experiment lasting only 96 h may indicate a more than additive joint action within this time period. This can be visualized if the time scale in Fig. 6.2 is changed to days instead of hours. Again, this demonstrates the importance of continuing an experiment until a threshold LC_{50} can be established so that the whole pattern of the response can be seen.

Sub-lethal effects

Almost all the research on the effect of mixtures of chemicals on fish has concentrated on mortality as the response. Some studies have been made using sub-lethal responses such as growth and reproduction, but these lack the precision necessary for a proper evaluation of the data and the results tend to be equivocal. Better results may be obtained with certain species of invertebrates such as Daphnia (the water flea) for which these effects can be measured with greater precision.

However, there is considerable scope for further research in this field; in particular, there is increasing interest in grouping chemicals according to their mode of toxic action as shown by their effect on various physiological reactions in fish. Such studies, together with those concerning the effects of chemicals on fish at the cellular level of organization, may further improve our fundamental understanding of the effects of mixtures.

TOXICITY OF COMPLEX EFFLUENTS

Most of the studies on mixtures have been made with pure chemicals or with pesticide formulations; very little has been published on the effects of individual chemicals within complex effluents, such as those arising from sewage treatment works which receive a mixture of domestic and industrial wastes. It is common practice to control these effluents on the basis of the major known contaminants − for example, suspended solids, ammonia and heavy metals − without checking whether these are potentially the most harmful to fish in the receiving water. If toxicity tests are carried out, the results are generally expressed in terms of the overall toxicity of the effluent, and no attempt is made to identify the relative importance of the individual constituents. Occasionally, attempts are made to fractionate an effluent into different components and to test these separately, and this can have some value. A review of the problems associated with assessing the toxicity of complex effluents is given in Bergman *et al.* (1986).

An alternative approach is to compare the toxicity curve for the effluent with those obtained for the individual constituents. For example, if the toxicity curve obtained for an effluent is identical to that for non-ionized ammonia, and the concentration of non-ionized ammonia in the dilution of effluent at the threshold LC_{50} is the same as that for non-ionized ammonia alone, then it is reasonably safe to assume that the toxicity of the effluent is primarily due to ammonia.

Furthermore, experience with mixture toxicity would suggest that no other harmful chemicals are present at concentrations greater than 0.2 TU in the effluent dilution corresponding to the threshold LC_{50}. Therefore, if the concentration of ammonia was considerably reduced, the toxicity of the effluent will be reduced by at least five-fold.

Use of TUs in pollution control

There have been some suggestions that the concept of TUs can be used to identify the relative importance of several effluents discharged into a short stretch of a watercourse. For example, if the threshold LC_{50} for an effluent corresponds to a five-fold dilution, then it contains 5 TUs per unit volume (e.g. 1 litre). Therefore, if 100 000 litres are discharge in a day, the contribution of that effluent is 500 000 TUs. Similar calculations can be made for the other effluents discharged to a nearby area. This can help to quantify the relative risks associated with the discharge of low volumes of highly toxic effluents and high volumes of effluents of low toxicity. Estimates can also be made of the total toxic load discharged to this watercourse by summing the TUs in the various effluents, although this will overestimate the dilution required to render them harmless because it is likely that the combined action will be less than additive.

However, there have been two major constraints in the development of the use of such an approach for pollution control:

- There are strict regulations governing the use of fish for experimental purposes,
- Few local regulatory authorities have the resources to carry out toxicity tests.

In addition, because every effluent is unique in its composition, the results of any test carried out are used mainly for internal operational controls by the industry. Therefore, the data are unlikely to be published in the scientific literature and are thus not available for testing the various hypotheses for mixture toxicity. However, with the greater understanding of the scientific basis for the difference in sensitivity between organisms to chemicals, it may be possible to use invertebrates as test organisms and to extrapolate from these results to predict the potential effects of complex effluent discharges on fish in the receiving water.

CONCLUSIONS

It is clear that more research is required on the theoretical basis of the toxicity of mixtures to fish in order to understand and predict the potential harmfulness of complex wastes such as sewage effluents. However, the results of the studies to date indicate that synergism is most unlikely to occur; the joint action is likely to be additive or less than additive. This has considerable significance for the setting and use of water quality standards described in the Chapter 7.

7 Development of Water Quality Standards to Protect Fish

The driving force of much of the research outlined in the previous chapters has been the need to determine the concentration of chemicals that, unless exceeded, will not cause harm to fish. This forms the basis of the derivation of water quality standards, as described in previously cited reviews (EIFAC and Water Research Centre reports; Alabaster & Lloyd, 1982; Howells *et al.* 1990). This chapter outlines some of the principles and problems associated with the setting of such standards.

THE WORK OF EIFAC

As far as some of the common polluting chemicals are concerned, identifying the concentration of a given chemical which, if exceeded, will cause harm to fish, is not a simple matter. This has already been made clear. There are many factors that can affect the toxicity of chemicals and these have to be taken into account, not only in the design of the experiment and the reporting of results, but also in the formulation of water quality standards to protect fish.

In the late 1950s, reviews were made of the published literature on the effects of chemicals on fish but the data reported were limited to the species tested, the duration of exposure and the concentrations found to be harmful. The examination of the literature was uncritical. Indeed, there are many compilations of toxicity data to this day which have been abstracted from research papers without a critical analysis of the validity of the experimental methods or of the results obtained. These compilations do not provide the basis for setting water quality standards, but only a starting point for a literature search.

However, in 1960 the Food and Agriculture Organization of the United Nations set up the European Inland Fisheries Advisory Commission (EIFAC) as a regional body, and, in response to the recognized need for the effective control of pollution to protect fisheries, a Working Party on Water Quality Criteria for European Freshwater Fish was formed in 1962. The function of this Working Party was to select specific substances which were known to have caused damage to fisheries is European rivers, and to make a critical review of all the pertinent literature in order to derive appropriate water quality criteria or standards.

It was agreed by the Working Party at the outset that:

'Water quality criteria for freshwater fish should ideally permit all stages in the life cycle to be successfully completed and, in addition, should not produce conditions in a river water which would either taint the flesh of the fish or cause them to avoid a stretch of river where they would otherwise be present, or give rise to accumulation of deleterious substances in fish to such a degree that they are potentially harmful when consumed. Indirect factors like those affecting fish-food organisms must also be considered should they prove to be important.'

Therefore the main emphasis was on the protection of fish, and other aquatic organisms were taken into account when deriving standards only if they were an important and irreplaceable component of the diet of fish.

The need for critical reviews

The emphasis on a critical review of the literature meant that each report had to be drafted by an expert with proven research experience on the substance being considered. Every published paper was carefully assessed in the light of the current state of knowledge on the subject, and the authors were approached for further information when this was necessary. Experience showed that the author's conclusions which were drawn from the experimental results were not always correct, either because of a faulty experimental technique or because factors later shown to be important were not taken into account. As stated earlier, most published papers are refereed by experts, but some unsatisfactory studies can slip through the net, or become subsequently outdated. For these reasons the conclusions of the author cannot be accepted without question; this problem has been reviewed by Lloyd (1986).

One outcome of this approach was that progress in producing water quality criteria for the important pollutants was necessarily slow; over the next 28 years water quality criteria documents were published for 14 substances, even though in later years the initial drafts were prepared by a small team of scientists with expertise on separate aspects of the problem. To some extent the slow progress reflected the choice of the substances studied in that, because of their recognized importance, there was a considerable amount of information published on their effects, all of which had to be critically assessed. Also, as the years progressed, the amount of information available increased rapidly as more resources were allocated to pollution research.

Scope of the reviews

The scope of these critical reviews included:

(1) Information on the sources from which the substance could enter watercourses,
(2) Laboratory data on the mode of toxic action, lethal and sub-lethal effects and the various factors that influence toxicity (as described in previous chapters),
(3) Field observations of polluted rivers and the concentrations that caused accidental fish kills,

(4) The effects on aquatic invertebrates and plants.

Of the above, the emphasis on the results of field studies was probably the most important because of the commonly held opinion that laboratory studies cannot mimic the complex interactions that occur in natural waters. Laboratory experiments are designed to study the effect of changing one variable at a time, whereas all the variables are constantly changing in 'real life' and interactions within communities of organisms may be important factors in determining the harmful effects of a chemical in practice.

Assessment of field data

Experience has shown that good field data on the effects of individual substances on fish to support proposed water quality standards are rare. The main exception is for the heavy metals which are the sole pollutants in remote lakes and streams that drain old mining areas, as found in parts of Wales and Norway. Providing that the concentrations of metals do not fluctuate too widely, the information on the status of the fish populations along a gradient of pollution in these waters can be used as strong supporting evidence for a proposed water quality criterion.

For other substances the normal situation is more complex. It is rare to find, for example, a river where the only pollutant is ammonia; usually, other potentially harmful substances are present which may contribute to the observed status of the fish population. Furthermore, long experience of field studies which have been undertaken to correlate measured concentrations of pollutants in the water with effects on fish held in cages has shown that unforeseen episodic events can have an overriding effect. These events can arise from sporadic discharges of effluents directly to a river or via a sewage treatment works and it is possible that in many areas the actual status of the fish populations is much more a reflection of the frequency and severity of these episodes and not the underlying baseline level of contamination. In these situations, therefore, the absence of a flourishing fish community cannot be attributed to the concentration of a substance measured as part of a routine monitoring programme or a special survey. However, such monitoring and survey data do show what concentrations of substances can be present and also which of them do not have an apparent effect on fish populations, and this can be valuable information. Even so, the data have to be examined carefully to find out whether the populations have been acclimated to the pollutant or whether reproduction has been affected and the population is sustained by immigration of juveniles from outside the area. Despite these shortcomings, the inclusion of field evidence into the critical assessment of the data has been found to provide an essential support for the formulation of water quality standards to protect fish.

Fish food organisms

Experience has also shown that fish populations are seldom affected because their supply of food organisms is reduced; an exception is the reduction in benthic fauna in streams polluted by suspended solids such as china clay wastes which form a blanket on the substrate. Otherwise, the removal of sensitive species and their replacement by similar, more resistant, organisms does not affect the quantity of food available to the fish. Therefore, water quality standards set to protect fish will not automatically protect all other aquatic life; in general, more stringent standards are required for this purpose.

Validity of EIFAC water quality criteria

Although progress on developing the EIFAC criteria has been slow, the outcome has been a set of defensible water quality standards which have been incorporated into national legis-

lation and, with minor modifications, into the EEC Directive
on water quality requirements for freshwater fish (EEC 1978),
as summarized in Table 8.1. Despite the natural caution
expressed by the authors of the various reports in putting
forward 'tentative' water quality criteria, information obtained
and published in later years tends to support the accuracy of
the proposed numerical standards rather than suggesting that
they are in error. There is no doubt whatsoever that for these
common pollutants a critical review of all the work published
on laboratory and field studies can be used as a basis for the
formulation of accurate water quality standards to protect
fish.

WATER QUALITY CRITERIA FOR LESS COMMON CHEMICALS

During the past 40 years, there has been a steady increase in
the number of chemicals produced by industry, together with
an increase in the tonnage used. At the same time, methods
of chemical analysis have improved so that very small concentrations can be detected in water. But unlike the common
pollutants, very few of these have been directly implicated as
the cause of chronic pollution in surface waters. This general-
ization applies even to pesticides. As a result, there is much
less laboratory data available on the effects of these chemicals
on fish, and field data are almost non-existent. It is clear that
in these circumstances the setting of water quality standards
becomes more difficult.

Use of limited data

For most chemicals, and certainly for all new chemicals, data
exist on their acute toxicity to at least one species of fish. For
some of the commoner chemicals there may be such information on their toxicity to several species and in rare cases
the results of a longer term experiment. In these cases the
first step is to obtain a crude estimate of their potential harm-

fulness to fish. The basis of this assessment is a comparison between the concentration of the chemical that causes toxicity and the concentration to which the fish is likely to be exposed in the aquatic environment. In some cases an initial crude assessment is sufficient; for example, a chemical with a 96 h LC_{50} of 1 gm/l (and with evidence that this is a threshold concentration) and a predicted maximum concentration in water of 1 µg/l, that is, one million times lower, is most unlikely to be a cause of harm to fish because of the large margin of safety.

However, as the gap between these two values narrows, more accurate estimations of the relevant concentrations have to be made — estimates for example, of the relationship between the sensitivity of the test species of fish for which the acute toxicity data was obtained and the most sensitive fish species, and the relationship between the acute toxic concentration and the concentration that will not cause harm to the species tested. These relationships can be expressed as numerical 'application' factors; for example, an application factor of 0.1 might be applied to a threshold 96 h LC_{50} to derive the maximum concentration that does not cause harm to the particular species used in the test.

Appropriate application factors

There have been many attempts to derive appropriate application factors (also known as 'uncertainty' factors) by reviewing all the relevant information available on the relationship between the concentration causing acute toxicity and the concentration at which no harmful effects are observed. However, some of these contain fundamental errors, the most basic being in the relationship between the 96 h LC_{50} and the 'safe' concentration. It is clear that for those chemicals that have a linear toxicity curve, the safe concentration will be much lower than the 96 h LC_{50} (that is, the application factors will be smaller) than those for which the 96 h LC_{50} is a threshold concentration.

Therefore, the size of this application factor must be linked to the shape of the toxicity curve, otherwise all chemicals will be treated as if they had the long-term potential for harm of the highly toxic and bioaccumulating pesticides. Indeed, the large amount of information on the lethal and sub-lethal effects of such pesticides tends to dominate any such review of the available literature. There is no reason to suppose that the application factor of 0.05−0.10, derived for the common pollutants for which there is a sufficiently extensive data base, should not be applicable to the threshold LC_{50}s obtained for other chemicals with similar toxic properties.

Similarly, the application factors required to allow for differences in species sensitivity have been based on data obtained for chemicals with differing modes of toxic action; this error is more serious when deriving application factors to protect aquatic life in general because the inclusion of data for pesticides which by definition are much more toxic to some species than to others leads to an overestimate of the appropriate factor.

QUANTITATIVE STRUCTURE ACTIVITY RELATIONSHIPS (QSARs)

Considerable advances have been made in recent years in the techniques used to predict the behaviour of chemicals in the environment from an analysis of their molecular structure and associated physico-chemical properties. For example, these properties can be used to predict the likelihood of a chemical occurring in natural waters in significant quantities. There is a rapidly expanding literature on this subject; a useful introduction to this field is provided by Kaiser (1984, 1987).

Use of QSARs to predict toxicity

One of the more important aspects of these studies, in the context of this chapter, has been the provision of a greater understanding of the toxicity of those chemicals that have a physical toxic action on the cell membranes of organisms. One of the basic factors that govern the toxicity of these chemicals is their solubility in fat. A chemical that has similar properties to fat is n-octanol; if a chemical is placed in a vessel containing water and n-octanol, its distribution between these two liquids can be measured and the ratio of the con-centrations is known as the n-octanol water partition co-efficient. Because this can be a high number, it is usually expressed as a logarithm, i.e. log K_{ow} or log P_{ow}, P or K referring to the partition, and o and w to octanol and water. The higher the log K_{ow} of a chemical, the greater its potential to accumulate in the fatty tissues of fish; therefore the con-centration of such a substance in water that will result in a certain level of accumulation in fish is much less than for those chemicals with a low log K_{ow}.

The toxicity of these chemicals is thus correlated with their log K_{ow}. However, for substances with a complex molecular structure there are other physico-chemical factors which can affect the toxicity and these have to be taken into account. Furthermore, although the log K_{ow} gives an indication of the potential of a chemical to accumulate in fatty tissues, in practice the fish may be able to metabolize and detoxify the chemical so that such an accumulation does not occur. Thus, the stage has not been reached when the toxicity of an organic chemical can be predicted from its molecular structure with complete confidence.

However, if the threshold LC_{50}s for a group of chemicals and one species of fish is shown to be correlated with their respective log K_{ow}s, as shown in Fig. 7.1, then it can be assumed that their toxic actions are identical. This could lead to a solution of the problem of making a hazard assessment for those chemicals with little toxicity data, because all the data for the chemicals within this common group (or homo-logous series) can be combined after allowance for differences in the log K_{ow}. For example, the relationship between the threshold LC_{50} and the safe concentration derived for one of the chemicals should apply to all the others; similarly, the

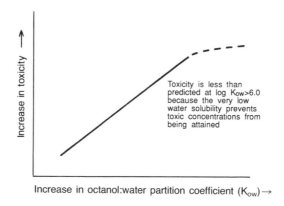

Fig. 7.1 Relationship between the octanol:water partition coefficient of chemicals with a simple narcotic toxic action and their toxicity to fish.

differences in species sensitivity should be common for all the chemicals, not only for fish but perhaps also for other aquatic organisms. For example, it is possible that the eco-toxicological data for benzene, toluene and xylene may be capable of being combined in this way. This will make the task of deriving defensible water quality criteria easier.

It should be remembered, however, that all chemicals with a physical toxic action are additive in their joint toxicity, so that any water quality standards for such chemicals singly will have to be reduced if there are significant concentrations of others in the water.

Implications for water quality criteria

If the above analysis of the situation is correct, then the need to carry out an extensive series of toxicity tests on new sub-stances may well be reduced. For example, the sensitivity of fish to a chemical may be inferred from data for an invertebrate species such as Daphnia if proof is obtained that the substance belongs to a homologous group with a common QSAR. Although the use of QSARs can help to make a more accurate prediction of the concentrations of physically toxic chemicals that are harmful to fish and to other aquatic life, there may still be a considerable gap between these levels and those found in the field. Therefore, field data cannot be used to support or refine the accuracy of a water quality standard which has been predicted only from laboratory data.

This then leads to another problem: at what concentration should the water quality standard be set? For example, if the maximum concentration of chemical A which causes no harm to fish is 1.0 mg/l, and the maximum concentration recorded in a watercourse is 1.0 μg/l, then the water quality standard can be set somewhere between these two values. But if it is set at the higher end of the range, then the implication is that environmental concentrations can be considerably increased and this may be politically unacceptable; and if it is set at the lower end, then the implication is that the chemical is much more toxic than the laboratory evidence suggests and that if this standard is exceeded on a rare occasion, then fish in that stretch of water are endangered. This dilemma will be referred to again in Chapter 8.

EXPRESSION OF THE WATER QUALITY STANDARD

Throughout the preceding chapters, considerable emphasis has been given to the fluctuations that occur in the concentrations of a chemical entering the water, and in the various factors that affect their toxicity. It is clear that the main objective for the protection of fisheries is to control the inputs so that peak concentrations do not persist for long enough to harm fish. But it is also clear that this objective cannot be translated into a numerical standard which embraces a maximum concentration and a duration of exposure because this would require a continuous chemical monitoring of the waterbody.

Use of average values

On the other hand, a standard expressed as an average concentration may be inappropriate because it does not allow for the wide fluctuations which may occur in practice during which levels may be reached that are harmful to fish. The exception to this is for standards for strongly bioaccumulating chemicals where the limiting values are based on concentrations in fish flesh in order to protect the consumer; in this case, a standard based on the average concentration to which the fish are exposed is an appropriate value for such chemicals, because the fish act as an integrator of the fluctuating concentrations in the water.

Use of the 95 percentile

For other chemicals, the average concentration has to be supplemented by another value that reflects the peak values which are acceptable. In the EIFAC standards, for example, this value is expressed as the 95 percentile, that is, the concentration that should not be exceeded in 95% of the samples taken from a station on the watercourse. This standard is usually based on data derived from laboratory tests and therefore represents the concentration that will not harm fish even after prolonged exposure. The expression of such a standard as a 95 percentile may err on the side of safety. An analysis of ways in which concentrations of chemicals fluctuate in rivers suggests that generally the 95 percentile value will be about 3−4 times higher than the corresponding average concentration; thus, if the average concentration of a chemical was 1 mg/l, then 95% of the samples would be below 3−4 mg/l. But clearly this relationship will vary with the nature of the discharge − whether it is continuous or intermittent − and with variations in the volume of dilution water available. For example, if a constant discharge is made into a lake in which the water has a long residence time, the concentrations there will show little variation. Similarly, concentrations in a chalk stream fed by spring water where there is little change in seasonal flows will also remain fairly stable. However, concentrations in a flashy river where the flows fluctuate widely with the rainfall will show a considerable variation. For this reason the 95 percentile is a more acceptable expression of water quality standards, with the corresponding average value depending on the nature of the waterbody to which the discharge is made.

Nevertheless, standards based on a 95 percentile give rise to other problems, in particular that of proving that the standard has been met. At its simplest, a standard expressed as a 95 percentile has been taken to imply that out of 12 monthly samples taken at a sampling point during a year, 11 must meet this value and even if one sample fails, the standard is met. This is the loose interpretation made in the EEC Directive for the protection of freshwater fish (EEC 1978) and it is one of practical convenience. However, there is no upper limit on the extent to which the single sample is allowed to fail and therefore a single accidental discharge of a chemical which produces a harmful peak concentration, even if it coincides with a sampling time, may not cause that stretch of river to fail the standard.

A more statistical approach is to examine the distribution of the numerical values obtained for a chemical in samples taken throughout the year and estimate whether the 95 percentile standard has been met. The advantage of using a calculated approach is that other factors such as the accuracy of the analytical technique and the extent to which a few spot samples can reflect the annual water quality conditions can be taken into account. However, these calculations can only be made after the end of the year, and the proof of compliance with a standard can become clouded by the statistical approach used; the result will be expressed as the probability that the standard has, or has not, been met. Although this may reflect the reality of the situation, it does not help with the problem of enforcement.

The alternative compromise is to set a maximum concentration that should not be exceeded in any sample. This has the benefit of simplicity and it allows the possibility of immediate regulatory action. Also, it can be applied to situations where only a few samples are taken in any one year and where there is a seasonal pattern of sampling associated with discharges that occur only at certain times during the year.

Use of combined average and maximum values

The combination of an average and a maximum value is probably the best solution available. It is not, however, without its hidden drawbacks. If a sample is analysed for a chemical and a high concentration is found, there are two possible causes. The sample may have been taken at a time when a sporadic peak concentration was present in the water and it is therefore a true value. Alternatively, the sample bottle may have been contaminated or an error made during the analysis. By the time the high value is noted, the original sample may have been discarded, and a fresh sample from the river station may show a normal concentration if the peak has passed.

If there was no apparent untoward occurrence observed at the station at the time of sampling (e.g. a fish mortality or a discoloration of the water) the analyst is in a dilemma. If the high value is entered into the records, there may be subsequent doubts about its validity; there could be a temptation to discard the result especially if it makes a substantial difference to the average annual value calculated for that year, suggesting that a marked reduction in river quality has occurred even though other evidence shows that this was unlikely. The easiest course would be not to record the result and to take another sample. Obviously, such an action would be against the procedures laid down for the conduct of the sampling programme; nevertheless, it is possible that a few sporadic discharges go unrecorded in this way.

CONCLUSIONS

These examples show the importance of setting water quality standards in such a way that the normal chemical monitoring programmes can readily demonstrate whether or not the standard has been met. They also show the difficulty in achieving this aim, in particular because of the inability of a normal routine sampling programme to adequately describe the fluctuating levels of chemicals, and the other factors that affect their toxicity (e.g. the factors that affect ammonia toxicity), in the aquatic environment. The integration of water quality standards into a pollution prevention policy to protect freshwater fish is described in Chapter 8.

8   Protection of Freshwater Fish

Previous chapters have described the scientific basis for the development of water quality standards to protect fish, using information on the concentration-effect relationships obtained for specific chemicals. In this chapter, the problems of putting these standards into effect will be outlined. More detailed information can be obtained from standard works on water pollution law; in particular, the impact of EEC legislation on UK practices has been described by Haigh (1987). There are several other measures that are used for the prevention and control of pollution and these will be reviewed in the specific context of the protection of freshwater fish.

HISTORICAL BACKGROUND

For centuries, freshwater fish have been protected as a resource, initially because their value as a food for man and animals led to overfishing. In the reign of Elizabeth I a law was passed to prevent the over-exploitation of coarse fish as a source of food for pigs, and there were many restrictions on the taking of salmon, trout and eels. It was not until the mid-19th century that the polluted state of rivers which drained the expanding industrial areas became a cause of public concern. This led to a number of initiatives in the UK including the setting up of Royal Commissions to investigate the problem and the passing of legislation. The first attempt to protect fish from pollution seemed simple. The Salmon and Freshwater Fisheries Act of 1886 contained the clause:

'No person shall cause or knowingly permit to flow, or put or knowingly permit to be put, into any waters containing fish, or into any tributaries thereof, any liquid or solid matter to such an extent as to cause the waters to be poisonous or injurious to fish or the spawning grounds, spawn or food of fish, and if any person contravenes this subsection he shall be guilty of an offence against this Act: ...'

This clause was repeated in the subsequent Acts of 1923 and 1975, with the proviso that a person was not liable to a penalty if the discharge was authorized and if he could prove:

'that he had used the best practicable means, within a reasonable cost, to prevent such matter from doing injury to fish or to the spawning grounds, spawn or food of fish; ...'

These clauses show that there was a firm intention to protect fish, while recognizing the need for discharges to be made to watercourses. But in practice these clauses were difficult to enforce. In rivers receiving multiple inputs it was difficult to prove that any one discharge was the specific cause of harm to a fishery, and even if it were, then there was always the defence that remedial action to improve the discharge would be too expensive, and in times of intense industrial competition, recession and unemployment, such arguments would be very persuasive.

In practice, the use of Common Law was more effective; a riparian owner had a reasonable expectation that his waters should contain a flourishing fish population and deserved compensation if upstream discharges prevented the establishment of this resource. It was in recognition of such an expectation that the Anglers' Co-operative Association (ACA) was formed in 1948 and in the following years a considerable number of successful prosecutions were brought against dischargers of harmful effluents. The ACA is supported entirely by anglers' voluntary subscriptions and so represents the public concern for the maintenance and restoration of freshwater fisheries. However, it is clear that for over 100 years there has been a recognition in successive Acts of Parliament that freshwater fish should be protected from pollution. The main problem has been in the enforcement of this intention and, during this century, there has been a steady progress towards the development of water quality standards for substances in effluents and in rivers.

The 'Royal Commission' standards

It was recognized in the early years of this century that numerical standards should be used to limit the amount of potentially polluting substances discharged to surface waters. In the Eighth Report of the UK Royal Commission on Sewage Disposal (1912) it was stated that:

> 'A chemical standard may be applied in one of two ways — either to the contaminating discharge by itself, or to the stream which has received the discharge. Since our main objective is primarily the improvement of rivers, and only secondarily the improvement of effluents, it would seem logical that standards should be applied not to sewage liquors or effluents alone but to such discharges under ordinary conditions, i.e. when mixed with river water.'

This Commission had surveyed a selection of rivers in the UK, and came to the conclusion that a watercourse would ordinarily be free from signs of pollution if the biochemical oxygen demand (BOD) of the water did not exceed 4.0 ppm in five days; if this value was exceeded then there would be signs of pollution except perhaps in very cold weather. This was a crude rule of thumb approach; it took no account of the rates of re-aeration of the water which are higher in fast flowing rivers than in slow, and so it did not necessarily reflect the amount of dissolved oxygen in the water. Also, the 'signs of pollution' was a subjective assessment. Nevertheless, this was a major step forward with the resources available at that time.

The major consequence of this conclusion was the setting of effluent standards for sewage disposal works. The Commission found that the normal background BOD of river water was 1.5 ppm, so that an increment of 2.5 ppm could be allowed without visible signs of pollution occurring. If the sewage effluent received a minimum dilution of eight-fold after discharge, then its BOD should not be greater than 20 ppm if the increment of 2.5 ppm in the rivers is not to be exceeded. If the dilution was considerably in excess of eight-fold, then this effluent standard could be relaxed, providing that the extra BOD input did not cause that of the river to exceed 4.0 ppm.

This approach became a basic principle that was applied to pollution control measures in subsequent years. Water quality standards could be set for surface waters, and in some cases these could be varied according to the sensitivity of the resource or use that needed protection. The standards applied to effluents discharged to these waters were set on a case-by-case basis so that if they complied the water quality standard would not be exceeded.

However, this Royal Commission made a second recommendation to the effect that the suspended solids content of a fully treated effluent should not exceed 30.0 ppm. There were no quantitative field data to support this standard as there were for the BOD. However, the Commission noted that the suspended material could settle out downstream of the discharge and cause a nuisance but because of differences in river flows and in the nature of the substrate, the degree of pollution caused was very variable. Therefore, a standard was set which reflected the normal performance of a well-run sewage disposal works; it was based on what could be achieved by the treatment processes used, rather than on the quality requirements of the receiving water.

Pollution controls to protect fish

At the beginning of this century, then, the basic principles of pollution control were beginning to crystalize. These principles can be summarized as follows in the context of the protection of freshwater fish:

(1) Water quality standards can be set to protect fish,
(2) Effluent standards can be set to ensure that the water quality standards in the receiving water are not exceeded,
(3) Effluent standards can be set on the basis of the performance of the best treatment plant available, taking into account the economic feasibility of such processes,
(4) A general requirement can be established that freshwater fish should be protected.

Although it would seem logical to place the last item at the top of the list, in practice it is easier to follow the development of these principles in the order given. It should also be remembered that the main thrust of this development and the associated research was to restore the fishless rivers to a condition where a reasonable fishery could become re-established.

PRESENT LEGAL FRAMEWORK OF WATER QUALITY STANDARDS

It comes as some surprise that the Royal Commission's observation that waters with a BOD in excess of 4.0 ppm were polluted, did not produce an incentive to establish standards for other potentially polluting chemicals. This was largely the result of the nature of UK legislation in which the Acts state the general intention and subsequent regulations are made to ensure that these intentions are fulfilled. But is also reflects the difficulty of establishing scientifically sound criteria, as has been shown in the previous chapters.

It was not until the middle of this century that the necessary research programmes gathered momentum and even then the water quality requirements for fish could be expressed only as tentative standards. These standards had to conform to reality;

the presence of a good fishery in a river where the water quality standard for a certain chemical was not met would destroy the credibility of that standard in a court of law.

However, it is not UK practice to enshrine water quality standards in pollution control legislation. Instead, the regional regulatory authority can set conditions for the quality of the effluents discharged to their waters and it is these consent conditions that are legally enforceable.

Appropriate legislation came into force in 1951 and has been developed in subsequent Acts. The general feeling of the legislators at that time was that the precise relationship between water quality and water use (e.g. protection of fisheries) was subject to so much local variation that no national standards could be set. While this is certainly true for some of the common pollutants, as described in earlier chapters, it is surprising that the well-established Royal Commission standards for BOD and suspended solids were not given legal status. As a result, there is scope for considerable flexibility in setting of consents for effluent discharges, leading in some cases to accusations of laxity in pollution prevention.

The changing pattern of effluent composition

To some extent, this flexible approach may have been influenced by the changing nature of the pattern of effluent discharges. In the 1950s, it soon became clear that it would be difficult to make the necessary improvements to many of the small industrial discharges because of the lack of space available for treatment plants, especially in the large towns and cities where the factories and houses were tightly packed together. The solution to this problem was to divert such effluents to the sewers so that they could be treated in conjunction with domestic sewage at the local treatment works. Payment is made for this treatment, and conditions placed on the discharges to ensure that they do not have a harmful effect on the sewage treatment processes, nor cause the conditions set for the sewage effluent to be exceeded. Therefore, the scene changed from a situation where there was a multiplicity of small discharges into rivers draining industrial areas, to one where there are a much smaller number of sewage works discharging effluents containing the residues of many industrial wastes. Added to this was the development of trunk sewers in many catchment areas so that small treatment works in the headwater regions could be closed down and the sewage treated in much larger and efficient works situated further downstream. Although this undoubtedly improved the quality of freshwater, there were some industrial areas where the very high proportion of industrial wastes in the sewage had an adverse effect on the treatment processes, and accidental spillages of extremely toxic wastes could put the treatment plant out of action. It is possible that amid this changing scene the need for statutory water quality standards received a low priority.

EC Directives

In other countries the structure of their legislation made it easier to set environmental quality standards and in the early 1970s the Commission of the European Community embarked on a programme to harmonize the values set for specific water uses − drinking water supplies, freshwater fisheries, shellfisheries and bathing.

The Freshwater Fish Directive

The Freshwater Fish Directive (EEC 1978) was agreed by the Council of Environment Ministers in 1978 and came into operation two years later. As described earlier, the water quality standards were largely based on the critical reviews made by EIFAC but some deviations were made to accommodate the existing standards that were already in operation in member countries. These standards are listed in Table 8.1; it can be seen that only a limited number of substances are included, but these include the major causes of pollution in European waters as identified by EIFAC member states. It

Table 8.1 EC Directive for the protection of fish: digest of water quality standards

Parameter	Salmonids	Cyprinids	Remarks
(1) Temperature (°C)	I. Increment above upstream temperature should not exceed 1.5°C at the edge of the mixing zone	3.0°C	Sudden variations in temperature should be avoided
	I. The temperature should not exceed 21.5°C at the edge of the mixing zone for more than 98% of the time	28°C	Regional derogations from this standard are permitted. Species that require cold water for reproduction are protected by an upper limit of 10°C during the breeding season
(2) Dissolved oxygen (DO) (mg/l O₂)	G. 50% of samples ≥9 100% of samples ≥7	G. 50% of samples ≥8 100% of samples ≥5	Sampling should reflect the daily variations in DO concentrations, and if a single sample *only* is taken it should be at a time when the concentration is expected to be low
	I. 50% of samples ≥9 If dissolved oxygen concentration falls to below 6 mg/l action must be taken to identify the cause and to take remedial action if appropriate	I. 50% of samples ≥7 4 mg/l	

Cyprinids – includes all non-salmonid species
G values – guidelines which should be achieved where possible
I values – imperative values which must be observed
Sample compliance – except where indicated, the standards must be attained in 95% of the samples. Samples should be taken at least monthly, unless the inputs are very small when a lower sampling frequency is acceptable

Table 8.1 (cont'd)

Parameter	Salmonids	Cyprinids	Remarks
(3) pH (units)	I. 6–9	I. 6–9	Man-made inputs should not cause the natural pH to vary by more than ±0.5, nor cause an unacceptable increase in the toxicity of those substances whose harmfulness varies with pH. Regional derogations are allowed for waters with high natural acidity or alkalinity
(4) Suspended solids (mg/l)	G. Average value ≤25		Regional derogations apply to rivers with a naturally high suspended solids content. High concentrations at time of floods can be excluded from the calculation of the average value
(5) Biochemical oxygen demand (BOD; mg/l O_2)	G. ≤3	G. ≤6	There was a considerable debate on the inclusion of this parameter; BOD itself is not harmful to fish. The harmfulness of low DO caused by a high BOD is covered by the DO parameter above
(6) Total phosphorus	No specific standards set		Inputs of phosphorus should be controlled to prevent eutrophication. Appropriate limits are suggested for lakes and rivers

(7) Nitrites (mg/l NO_2)	G. ≤0.01	G. ≤0.03	More recent research suggests that these standards may be too stringent. The toxicity of nitrite decreases as the chloride concentration of the water increases
(8) Phenolic compounds (mg/l C_6H_5OH)	G. Should not taint fish flesh		This subjective standard is appropriate for fish for human consumption, and not for the safety of fish. Chlorinated phenols are the main cause of taint
(9) Petroleum hydrocarbons	G. Should not form a film on the water surface, or a coating on banks or water body beds. Should not taint fish flesh. Should not cause harm to fish.		These qualitative statements reflect the difficulty of setting quantitative standards to control pollution by oil
(10) Non-ionized ammonia (mg/l NH_3)	G. ≤0.005 I. ≤0.025		Minor daytime peaks in concentration which exceed the I values may be acceptable
(11) Total ammonia (mg/l NH_4^+)	G. ≤0.04 I. ≤1.0	G. ≤0.2 I. ≤1.0	These standards reflect the effect of ammonia oxidation to nitrate on the DO of the water; also, as with phosphorus, the effect of added nitrogen on eutrophication. However, no standard was set for nitrate levels

Cyprinids – includes all non-salmonid species
G values – guidelines which should be achieved where possible
I values – imperative values which must be observed
Sample compliance – except where indicated, the standards must be attained in 95% of the samples. Samples should be taken at least monthly, unless the inputs are very small when a lower sampling frequency is acceptable

Table 8.1 (cont'd)

Parameter	Salmonids	Cyprinids	Remarks
(12) Total residual chlorine (mg/l HOCl)	I. ≤0.005		This standard refers to water with a pH of 6. Somewhat higher values are acceptable in more alkaline waters. Chlorinated effluents can be discharged from power station cooling towers and swimming pools
(13) Total zinc (mg/l Zn) Water hardness (mg/l CaCO$_3$)			This reflects the effect of water hardness on zinc toxicity, as described in Chapter 5.
10	I. ≤0.03	I. ≤0.3	
50	≤0.20	≤0.7	
100	≤0.30	≤1.0	
500	≤0.50	≤2.0	

(14) Dissolved copper
(mg/l Cu)

Water hardness (mg/l $CaCO_3$)		
G.	10	≤0.005
	50	≤0.022
	100	≤0.040
	300	≤0.112

As with zinc, the toxicity of copper is reduced as the water hardness increases, as described in Chapter 5. The Directive allows for less stringent standards in soft waters where less toxic organo-copper complexes can be formed. These standards were given 'G' status because of their late inclusion in the Directive, following the EIFAC review on copper published in 1976. They are similar in status, however, to the other 'I' values in this Directive, and not to the lower, more stringent, 'G' values to be achieved where possible

Cyprinids – includes all non-salmonid species
G values – guidelines which should be achieved where possible
I values – imperative values which must be observed
Sample compliance – except where indicated, the standards must be attained in 95% of the samples. Samples should be taken at least monthly, unless the inputs are very small when a lower sampling frequency is acceptable

was the original intention that this list would be expanded to include other chemicals as further critical reviews became available and scientifically based standards were proposed. Also, the existing standards could be reviewed in the light of new knowledge. This has not occurred, probably for two main reasons.

The first reason was that the Directive does not apply to all waters but only to those designated by individual member states as being in need of protection. Therefore the number and length of the rivers which were designated depended on the political pressure placed on the respective authorities by the public. There was no penalty in the Directive for those designated waters that failed to comply with the standards; the competent national authorities are required to take the appropriate action. Despite this, there was considerable reluctance on the part of member states to designate waters other than those that clearly met all the standards in the Directive and for which the requirement for regular water quality monitoring was then minimal. The EC Commission has to be provided with regular reports on the extent to which the designated waters have complied and this can be used to maintain political pressure, both to increase the lengths of river designated and to improve their quality, but these reports do not appear to be generally available. After an encouraging start this Directive appears to have faded into oblivion in several EC member states.

The second reason was the introduction of a Directive to control the discharge of hazardous chemicals to water. This is commonly called the Dangerous Substances Directive (EEC 1976).

The Dangerous Substances Directive
In contrast to the directives for the protection of specific water uses, EEC 1976 concentrates on limiting the discharge of individual chemicals to surface waters. The main thrust of this Directive is to set standards for effluents from specific sectors of industry, and this will be discussed later. But it also includes water quality standards, in some cases set indi-

vidually to protect specific uses but more usually expressed as a single concentration to protect all uses. The list of potentially dangerous substances is endless; at present there is a primary list of 132 chemicals and efforts are being made to identify which of these are the most important in terms of being highly toxic, persistent in the environment, and accumulated to high concentrations in organisms. Those chemicals such as mercury, cadmium and persistent organochlorine pesticides are obvious candidates and form the 'Black List' for which regulations have been agreed. In contrast to the Freshwater Fisheries Directive, the Dangerous Substances Directive applies to all waters and not just to those designated by member countries; to this extent it is a much more powerful instrument to protect fisheries. However, in practice the chemicals being considered for the 'Black List' are increasingly of lesser importance to fisheries than those included in the Freshwater Fisheries Directive which, like the EIFAC proposals, focused on those chemicals that were known to have caused harm to natural populations of fish.

This raises the problem, described in Chapter 7, of setting scientifically sound water quality standards for those chemicals with a limited data base of ecotoxicological information, and which are present in water at concentrations far below those shown to be harmful. If the experience gained with potentially harmful chemicals is used to set a realistic standard, then the implication might be that the environmental concentrations could be allowed to rise considerably without causing damage. In those countries where the definition of pollution is the presence of chemicals in the environment arising from man's activities, such an increase would be clearly unacceptable. Therefore there is political pressure to set the standards as low as possible and this has led to proposals of very large 'application' factors to reflect the uncertainty surrounding the information available and the possibility of subtle harmful effects being caused by low concentrations. One regrettable outcome of this debate is that the scientific credibility of well-founded standards can become undermined, even for those chemicals with well-established water quality criteria, by this apparent need for large safety factors to reflect uncertainties in the predictive capability of laboratory data.

There is another sub-set of chemicals that do not rate as dangerous under the criteria of this directive and which form the 'Grey List'. This includes substances such as zinc, copper and ammonia which are important for fisheries. Discharges of effluents that contain 'Grey List' chemicals are controlled so that national quality standards set for the receiving water are not exceeded. For those chemicals in this list which are included in the Freshwater Fisheries Directive, the water quality standards set to protect fish are taken from that directive. Similar standards for other substances on the list have been prepared, or are in preparation, by the Water Research Centre (see References).

Consequences of exceeding the standard

It will be recalled that in Fig. 2.2, Chapter 2, the environmental quality standard (EQS) to protect fish is set at the concentration above which there will be a significant risk of damage. Because of the difficulty of measuring the onset of such damage in a fishery amid all the other natural and man-made factors that affect fish populations, exceeding the standard can be taken as presumptive evidence that the fish are being harmed. However, if the water quality standard for a substance is set at a very conservative concentration, incorporating a large safety margin, then exceeding of the standard will not necessarily cause significant damage to the fishery.

There is a mistaken tendency these days to assume that all standards are set on the same scientific basis. For some substances, it may be necessary for very conservative standards to be accompanied by a secondary value that more truly reflects the boundary EQS as shown in Fig. 2.2. This would prevent the occurrence of any situations in which a decline in the status of a fishery is wrongly attributed to the presence of a substance with a conservative standard, allowing the real cause of the decline to remain undetected and therefore unremedied.

TECHNOLOGY-BASED EFFLUENT STANDARDS

It is scarcely surprising that, given the considerable complex problems involved in deriving water quality standards and in ensuring that they are met, more attention has been given recently to the use to standards that reflect the present state-of-the-art technology for waste treatment.

As shown earlier, there has been a long acceptance that unnecessary discharges should not be made to water; for example, the limitation set for suspended solids in sewage effluents of 30 ppm was based on the ability of a well-run treatment works to achieve this standard. As the technology of effluent treatment has improved over the years, so the ability of industry to meet water quality standards has increased. The scene has slowly shifted from the situation where an acceptable defence against a charge of causing pollution could be that the best practicable means had been employed to treat the effluent, to the situation where industry should use the best practicable means to treat its effluents irrespective of the needs of the receiving water. This not only satisfies those who apply the more stringent definition of pollution, but also ensures that all industries producing certain types of effluent have to abide by the same limitations; the economic advantage of an industry situated on a watercourse where the dilution available was more than adequate to accept an untreated effluent, would be lost. The same fixed emission standards (FES) apply to industries situated in head waters as to those on the lower reaches of major rivers.

The main thrust of the EC Directive on Dangerous Substances is to harmonize the standards applied to effluents containing 'Black List' substances so that the same restrictions apply throughout the community. To some extent the demonstration of compliance with these restrictions on effluent quality is much easier than with environmental monitoring where the concentrations of chemicals are subject to a much greater variation. It is clear that, for those substances that are very persistent in the environment and can build up in sediments and organisms, there is a pressing need to limit all discharges to the greatest degree possible; technology based standards are thus very appropriate. This need becomes less for those chemicals with a low persistence in water and which are less toxic to aquatic organisms. Nevertheless, there is some logic in applying the same effluent standards to all industries that produce similar toxic wastes, so that no one factory can gain an economic advantage over its competitors because of the location of its operation.

THE CONFLICT BETWEEN EQS AND FES APPROACHES

There has been a considerable debate, not only within the EC but also world-wide, on the relative merits of environmental water quality standards and fixed emission standards to control pollution. It has already been noted that this debate hinges to some extent on the definition of pollution used. As the public perception of pollution swings from the anthropogenic view point (i.e. safeguarding man's use of the environment) towards an ecocentric position, so the demand for a maximum reduction of chemical inputs will increase. At the extreme, this equates to a policy of 'zero discharge' of man-made chemicals into the environment. The argument for this approach is that all such inputs, no matter how small, will have an effect on organisms as shown in Fig. 2.2. It is difficult to establish whether or not these effects are harmful; therefore, the only safe approach is to prevent the possibility of effects. Clearly, zero discharge is impossible to achieve and it can only be a goal at which to aim.

It is evident that the two approaches of water quality standards and technology-based standards are not mutually exclusive; most countries employ a mixture of both in their regulations, generally reflecting the way in which their water pollution control measures have developed. It must be recognized that a comprehensive national monitoring programme to determine whether water quality standards are being met is very expensive and becomes even more so as the number of substances to be measured increase and the concentrations which are present become smaller. It is much less expensive simply to require industry to install the best possible treatment plant and to provide evidence that it is working properly.

Emphasis on emission controls

Therefore, the main difference between the pollution controls advocated by different countries is in the relative emphasis given to the two basic approaches. In some countries the main emphasis is on uniform emission standards but with regulations which prevent the establishment of industry in those areas where the effluent would adversely affect the uses of the receiving water. The main criticism of this approach is that it concentrates attention on individual fixed point inputs and neglects the possibility of multiple inputs into a river system. It also neglects the inputs from diffuse sources which may be equally or more important but which are more difficult to control.

Another draw-back is that there are limits to how often an industry can replace its treatment plant to keep up with new technological advances. Some guarantee has to be given for the acceptable life-span of new treatment plant, to allow the capital costs to be written off. Also, new technology is not always trouble-free, and breakdowns can have significant environmental consequences. However, many of our water pollution problems stem from out-dated and inefficient waste treatment processes, and also from poor control of processes within the industrial plant. A particularly common problem is the inadvertent discharge of wastes to surface drains, especially in old factories. Considerable improvements can be achieved by good housekeeping within the factory perimeter.

Emphasis on water quality standards

In other countries the main emphasis is on environmental water quality standards to protect water usage from inputs from all sources, but with restrictions placed on unnecessary discharges. For example, an industry should not be allowed to discharge chemicals up to the limit allowable by the water quality standard if the concentrations can be reduced by economically acceptable treatment processes. The main criticism levelled at this approach is that without stringent common standards on effluents the flexible approach can be a licence to pollute, and the profitability of industry takes precedence over the protection of the environment.

From the point of view of the fisheries manager, the main criterion is that the aquatic environment should be capable of supporting a flourishing community of fish species, and inputs of chemicals from all sources should be controlled so that their concentrations are below those that cause harm. Neither of the above approaches, singly or in combination, is wholly satisfactory in this respect, and there is a danger that the needs of fisheries will be lost in the heat of the political and scientific arguments.

MIXING ZONES

At this point it is necessary to consider another aspect of effluent discharges to watercourses. In many cases the quality of the effluent itself will not meet the standards set for the receiving water and so there will be a zone around or below the discharge point where harmful effects may occur. This is called the mixing zone; it should not be confused with the volume of water required to completely mix and dilute the effluent because this is a continuing process downstream of the discharge.

A leaflet giving guidelines for the definition and monitoring of mixing zones has been published by the Water Authorities Association (1986) which emphasizes the problems that occur in estuarial and coastal waters. Indeed, recent research has been focused on marine problems, although the general principles apply also to fresh water. A useful description of a marine problem has been given by Haig *et al.* (1989); a mathematical model for predicting the extent and characteristics of a mixing zone is given in Park & Uchrin (1988).

It is essential that the mixing zone should be kept as small as possible but in addition there are several criteria that should be met. From the fisheries viewpoint, the mixing zone should not prevent the passage of migratory fish and so ideally it should extend to no more than two-thirds the width of the river. It should not be an 'ecological desert'; although some sensitive aquatic organisms on the river bed may be harmed and perhaps lost, there should remain a sufficient diversity of species to form an acceptable basis of a food chain for fish. Fish and other aquatic organisms which may drift through the zone should not be irreversibly damaged; the water within the zone should not be so toxic as to cause the death of fish which may swim into the area.

To some extent the size of the mixing zone can be reduced by multiple discharge points to achieve a more rapid mixing of the effluent with the receiving water although this does not affect the total load discharged; all that is achieved is a number of small mixing zones within the river instead of a single large one. However, this remedy may prevent the occurrence of an unsightly plume downstream of the discharge. The size of an acceptable mixing zone is based on the quality and volume of the effluent, the quality and volume of the receiving water (including the existence of other mixing zones associated with other discharges), and the sensitivity of the local water uses. Once agreement has been reached on size, routine samples to check for compliance with the controls should be taken as close as possible to the boundary of the zone. This may not be simple in a river where the flows are subject to wide seasonal variations; sampling points are usually determined by their ready accessibility by road, for example at bridges over the river, and are not capable of variation. Indeed, this restriction on the location of sampling points may prevent the actual boundary of the mixing zone from being defined; predictions of its extent may have to be made on the basis of analytical data obtained from samples taken at some distance downstream.

It is clear that there are complex problems associated with mixing zones, but these should not prevent due recognition being given to the fact that they do exist and that they can form a potential danger to fisheries. In practice, the actual size or length of the zone may have to be calculated from data on the effluent quality and volume and receiving water characteristics, rather than being measured and monitored *in situ*. This implies that concentration-effect relationships for the substances in the effluent and the aquatic life below the discharge are known. Indeed, the whole concept of mixing zones depends on a knowledge of the appropriate water quality standards; the use of technology-based standards alone does not provide the necessary information.

HOW EFFECTIVE ARE THESE POLLLUTION PREVENTION MEASURES?

The effectiveness of the measures taken to protect fish from pollution hinges on two basic components:

- The ability to set valid environmental quality standards,
- The ability to measure whether these standards are being met.

Validity of the standards

It has been shown in previous chapters that reasonably accurate water quality standards can be set to protect fish for chemicals that have been the subject of considerable laboratory and field investigations. Studies on the toxicity of mixtures indicate that for those chemicals with different toxic action, concentrations which are below the water quality standard are not additive so that these values need not be adjusted if more than one potentially toxic chemical is present in a watercourse. A greater understanding of the mechanisms of toxic action may assist in the derivation of similar accurate standards for chemicals that have a narcotic action on fish. However, in this case there is a need to take into account the possibility of the combined action of several such chemicals in the water.

It has also been shown that tests on the toxicity of complex effluents can assist in the identification of dominant pollutants, and also contribute to an evaluation of the hazard of such discharges to fisheries in the receiving water. Again, the studies on the effects of mixtures of chemicals show that the combined effects of multiple discharges is unlikely to lead to synergistic effects when all the individual water quality standards are met.

Therefore, part of the hazard assessment procedure — the quantification of the effects of chemicals on fish — has been achieved with a reasonable degree of accuracy.

Environmental exposure: water

As shown in Chapter 7, there are considerable difficulties in establishing the concentrations of potentially harmful chemicals to which fish are exposed in the field. There are also problems in obtaining information on the actual chemicals in the water that are causing harm or are potentially harmful to fish. Although the compositions of most industrial discharges are known, at least for the major components, there are others whose major constituents may vary widely, for example in the manufacture of laboratory chemicals by batch processes. The setting of consents for such effluents is difficult, as is the monitoring of the receiving water for the presence of specific chemicals. Other chemicals may be inadvertently discharged and the example has been given of the pesticide tecnazene in effluents from potato washing operations. The presence of such chemicals in the environment is usually discovered by chance.

So far, the emphasis has been on the control of effluents discharged to watercourses, and the importance of diffuse inputs has received less recognition. The inputs which have the greatest potential to cause harm are pesticides and herbicides applied to land and which can be washed into watercourses after rainfall. This may in practice be a minor problem with modern pesticides that are readily degraded in the environment, in contrast to the problems posed by the highly persistent organochlorine compounds. Their occurrence in watercourses is likely to be sporadic, although those compounds that bind strongly to soil and are flushed into water on eroded particles may persist in sediments. Their subsequent uptake by benthic organisms and passage into the food chain needs further investigation.

Apart from pesticides, there are many other substances that can gain entry to water as a result of their use; for example, salt from roads in winter, de-icing compounds used on aircraft and runways, oil and tyre rubber in road drainage, as well as the spillages from road accidents. There are also the large number of chemicals used in the home; for example, detergents, disinfectants, plasticizers, and even paint-brush cleaners which are discharged into the domestic sewage and, because they are not controlled discharges, they can be regarded as diffuse inputs. Furthermore, many of these substances are adsorbed onto sewage sludge at the treatment works and may not be fully broken down into harmless components. The subsequent disposal of such sludge onto land may allow further aerobic decomposition to occur, but there will be a risk of these substances being leached into watercourses following rainfall. The problem then becomes similar to that of pesticides applied to land, but with the difference that sewage sludge contains a vast array of substances. It is clear that this is an area that requires further research.

Routine chemical monitoring of surface waters is directed towards those chemicals known to be present and which are approaching, within an order of magnitude, the concentrations known to be harmful. The frequency at which samples are taken is also linked to the extent to which the water is likely to become polluted; thus a watercourse receiving only a few minor discharges will be sampled less frequently than one receiving one or more major inputs of sewage effluent or industrial wastes. As shown earlier, the sporadic nature of intermittent sampling may not record the presence of isolated high concentrations of those chemicals included in the analytical programme.

Thus, a chemical monitoring programme has a limited value;

it records only the presence of a few chemicals and even the concentrations measured may not reflect the true levels to which fish are exposed. On the other hand, these concentrations may overestimate the real hazard; it was shown earlier that the daytime analysis of non-ionized ammonia may cause a bias towards higher average values than those present in practice, and the measurement of total concentrations of heavy metals will not allow for the proportion which is complexed or adsorbed and therefore less available for uptake by fish. These errors may lead to the wrong attribution of the cause of observed damage to a fishery.

Environmental exposure: sediments and organisms

Finally, freshwater monitoring programmes are almost always focused on the concentration of chemicals in the water. This reflects the needs of other water uses − for drinking by man and domestic animals, for irrigation and for water contact sports. Relatively little, if any, monitoring is carried out on contaminants in sediments, although this in part may reflect the difficulty in interpreting the results because of the scant amount of relevant ecotoxicological information available. The monitoring of fish tissues for bioaccumulated chemicals has been limited to specific problem areas and there is a need for such surveys to be extended in terms of the number of chemicals measured, the frequency of sampling and the number of rivers and lakes included in the programme.

Much more emphasis has been given to the monitoring of sediments and organisms in the marine environment because there the maintenance of healthy fish and shellfish stocks which can be safely consumed by man and other valued avian and mammalian predators is of much greater importance in comparison to other uses. This demonstrates that such monitoring is possible and it is probably only the cost, and perhaps also the conservatism of the monitoring agencies, which prevents its more widespread introduction to freshwaters.

Some of the advantages and limitations of chemical monitoring programmes have now been reviewed. They provide quantitative information about the substances known to be present; however, organisms in the water react to the totality of the harmful substances present and therefore they have the potential to provide a better measure of water quality. The ability to measure changes in the populations of benthic organisms, which provides information on the quality of the water, is described later in this chapter.

NOTIFICATION OF NEW CHEMICALS

So far, the emphasis has been on the control of chemicals that are already used and occur in surface waters. However, prevention is better than cure. The rapid rise in the number of new chemicals being developed and used in recent years has led to increasing concern about their environmental safety. As a result, schemes and legislation have come into force in order to prevent a repetition of such disasters as that which arose from the use and disposal of polychlorinated biphenyls (PCBs). These initiatives have led to the development of a complex system of toxicological and ecotoxicological test requirements in order to provide a basis for the assessment of the potential dangers posed by the use of new, and existing, chemicals. A comprehensive review of this field has been given by Richardson (1986).

Hazard and risk

The assessment made for a new chemical is based on its potential hazard and environmental risk. There are a number of different definitions of the terms 'hazard' and 'risk', with no general acceptance of any one of them. In this brief review, the term 'hazard assessment' will refer to the evaluation of the harmful properties of a substance, and 'risk assessment' to the probability that harmful concentrations will occur in the environment.

Hazardous properties of chemicals

An ecological hazard assessment of a chemical is based on three potentially harmful properties:

(1) Its toxicity to organisms,
(2) Its persistence in the environment,
(3) Its potential for bioaccumulation in organisms.

The basic toxicity test requirements are a 96 h LC_{50} for a species of fish and a 48 h EC_{50} for Daphnia (the water flea); tests on the toxicity to algae may also be required. These are held to be representative of the major divisions of vertebrates, invertebrates and plants; they are also representative of the major trophic divisions of primary producers, herbivores and carnivores. This basic set of data is required for the approval or registration of chemicals and products; the differences between the corresponding risk assessments of pesticides and of other chemicals will now be briefly reviewed.

Pesticides

Because of the concern expressed about the widespread use of persistent pesticides in the 1960s, registration schemes were set up in many countries. These have tended to develop in isolation, so that the detailed information requirements vary from country to country. In the UK, toxicity data for fish, daphnia and algae are a basic requirement although this can be modified according to the type of pesticide. For example, pesticides that are specifically effective against insects (such as the synthetic pyrethroids) will obviously pose a threat to similar aquatic species. Similarly, a selective herbicide may be potentially harmful to aquatic plants. Additional ecotoxicological data are usually requested on the basis of the type of target that the pesticide is designed to control. Persistence is sometimes more difficult to establish because the rate of chemical breakdown can vary between environmental compartments. For example, the breakdown of a pesticide by bacteria may occur readily in aerobic water and soil, but be very slow in anaerobic sediments (e.g. tributyl tin). Also, the chemical may form complexes with organic matter or adsorb on to sediment particles and then may be unavailable for uptake by organisms (e.g. paraquat, which binds very tightly to clay particles). This will have the same consequences as that of a chemical with a short persistence.

The potential for bioaccumulation can be predicted from the octanol:water partition coefficient, which is a measure of the relative solubility of the chemical in fat and water, and also from the shape of the toxicity curve (see Chapter 3, Fig. 3.2). If the substance is likely to have a bioaccumulation factor (the concentration in the organism divided by the concentration in the water) of 100−1000 or more, then further tests are carried out to determine whether this level of accumulation occurs in practice, or whether the organism can metabolize and excrete the chemical, so reducing the body concentrations.

The relative importance of these three hazardous properties can be modified when the risk assessment takes into account the possibility that significant quantities of the pesticide will reach watercourses. At one extreme, a pesticide used in limited quantities in greenhouses will be unlikely to reach the aquatic environment in significant quantities; at the other extreme are aquatic herbicides which are deliberately applied to water. In between are the pesticides applied to land. Those used in agriculture may leach into watercourses, but the amounts may depend on the type of soil and the pattern of rainfall. Herbicides used to control weeds on railways, and industrial and urban paved areas, may reach watercourses via surface drains.

Each pesticide is, therefore, unique in the way in which its various properties are important in the risk assessment. A critical evaluation of the data has to be made by experts in the relevant field before approval can be given to a pesticide for a specified use. Where there are uncertainties in the risk assessment, a 'worst case' scenario is usually adopted, leading to the incorporation of considerable safety factors.

However, the ongoing swing, evident since the 1970s, away

from an anthropocentric view of pollution (in which emphasis is placed on the protection of fish in the aquatic environment) towards an ecocentric view will produce pressure to consider the protection of all life in water. Coupled with the increasing public concern about the use of pesticides, and the increasingly sensitivity of methods of analysis which can detect the minutest traces in water, the pressure to reduce the amount of pesticides used will increase. However, as stated earlier, the approved uses of pesticides have not caused significant effects on fisheries, compared with other sources of pollution. Careless disposal of unused spray and half empty containers, and accidental discharges (especially in recent years of wood preservative from timber treatment works), have led to fish kills. A change in the processing of pesticide treated products can also lead to problems, as shown earlier in the case of tecnazene. But in general the controls have been effective. These controls are based on restrictions or ban on the use of the pesticide; the derivation of environmental quality standards are not appropriate because of the manner of use which lead to sporadic diffuse source inputs.

Other chemicals
The regulation of non-pesticidal chemicals presents a different type of problem. Public concern about the proliferation of new substances, together with evidence of widespread environmental contamination of persistent chemicals such as PCBs and dioxins, has led to the setting up of schemes for the notification of the hazardous properties of new chemicals. In 1979 a scheme was introduced in the form of a Directive (79/831/EEC) and this has been further developed during the succeeding years. Estimates vary concerning the number of chemicals at present in use, but an average value seems to be about 100 000. Very few of these have caused problems for freshwater fisheries. Because these chemicals have not been developed to kill organisms, and because of the large number of chemicals involved, the scrutiny given to these substances is not so detailed as that for pesticides.

Again, the same base set of data on acute toxicity to fish,

daphnia and perhaps algae are required. However, some short cuts may be viable. With our increasing knowledge of the reasons for the difference in sensitivity between species, and the development of QSARs to predict the toxicity of similar groups of chemicals, it is possible that the amount of toxicity testing required can be reduced.

As more becomes known about the cause of the difference in sensitivity of organisms to chemicals in the water, the need to choose species that represent these major divisions is becoming less important. To some extent, this follows the development of QSARs, particularly for those chemicals that have a physical mode of toxic action. However, although there are general guidelines provided for the way in which these tests should be carried out, there is still a need for an expert evaluation of the data obtained because of the many factors that can affect the result; some of these have been described by Lloyd (1986).

If a chemical is produced in large quantities, or is likely to reach water readily, then more extensive tests may be required including the measurement of sub-lethal effects. However, the results of these tests can do no more than identify the broad category of harmfulness into which the substance falls. Where such categories have been formulated, there has been a tendency for them to be rather narrowly banded; for example, chemicals with 96 h LC_{50}s greater than 1000 ppm are generally regarded as harmless, and values below 1 ppm are considered dangerous. In between, there may be three intermediate categories with a ten-fold concentration range. Therefore, a thousand-fold range separates harmless from dangerous, but the dangerous category will include chemicals whose toxicity lies within a ten-thousand-fold range or more.

Classification schemes

These categories can be incorporated into general classification schemes for chemicals. The simplest of these are based on the hazardous properties of toxicity, persistence and bio-accumulation. A really hazardous chemical would have a high ranking for all three properties; a chemical with a 96 h LC_{50} of just below 1 ppm, but with a very short environmental persistence and no potential for bioaccumulation, cannot properly be regarded as very hazardous. Therefore, a classification scheme has to attempt to integrate the three hazardous properties, but even the simplest scheme can produce a distorted comparison. More advanced classification schemes try to incorporate elements of risk assessment, such as the production volume of the chemical and its projected use, but these tend to increase the number of anomalies produced. Ideally, a separate risk assessment should be made for each chemical, as with pesticides, in order to identify those whose use may need to be controlled. If chemical surveys show that a hazardous concentration of a substance occurs in the environment, then toxicity tests have to be made to establish concentration-effect relationships and, if necessary, appropriate controls placed on the substance's use or discharge to water.

It is too early to judge the effectiveness of such notification and classification schemes in improving the aquatic environment; their main impact may be in the protection of human safety. However, there are some areas of chemical usage where a classification scheme has been used to encourage the replacement of products by less toxic ones which fulfil the same purpose, even though there may be no evidence of environmental damage caused by the original substance. Examples are the chemicals used in the oil exploration and exploitation industry and this represents a precautionary approach to environmental protection.

THE PRECAUTIONARY PRINCIPLE

So far, in describing the methods for controlling man-made inputs into freshwaters, I have highlighted the problems involved. None of the methods, individually or collectively, can be completely successful in preventing pollution; areas of uncertainty surround the type and value of information obtained by each method. The need for expert evaluation of the data can lead to disagreements because different scientists can view the same information in different ways. Politicians and the public can receive conflicting scientific opinions, sometimes masquerading as fact, which serve to accentuate the uncertainties and create confusion. All the assessments and evaluations can only be expressed in terms of the probability that the interpretation is correct; there is always an element of doubt that can be exploited by those of an opposite persuasion. This has contributed to a public scepticism of expert judgement which has been bolstered by a number of well-publicized examples; such examples have been particularly evident in the field of medicine, where initial assessments of product safety have sometimes been shown subsequently to be wrong.

These uncertainties have led to the development of the precautionary principle, which states that action should be taken to avoid damaging impacts on the environment wherever there are reasonable grounds for suspecting a causal relationship between a substance and a damaging impact. The replacement of hazardous chemicals by their less toxic equivalents, as described in the previous section, clearly comes within this principle. But there is considerable scope for a varied interpretation of what is a 'reasonable' ground for suspicion, and what is a damaging impact. If there are difficulties in distinguishing between a change in organisms (as measured at any level of biological organization) and harm, then any change can be interpreted as damage. With an ecocentric definition of pollution, this principle can be used to support the goal of 'zero discharge'. This places, in effect, a greater emphasis onto the use of technology-based standards which have been incorporated in a moderate version of the principle used for pollution control in the past. But an undue emphasis on precaution — one that disregards all the scientific evidence available — could lead to an unbalanced priority in pollution clean-up programmes and hence a potential squandering of scarce financial resources in reducing inputs that are un-important and neglecting those that are affecting valuable resources. Therefore it is essential that the primary need to protect the uses of water remains paramount and that the pollution control measures adopted should reflect this need. Any drift away from the application of water quality standards to protect fish, despite their imprecision, may erode the emphasis on the need to protect this resource and therefore should be discouraged.

BIOLOGICAL MONITORING PROGRAMMES

As stated earlier, it is certain that any man-made input into freshwaters will alter the natural balance of animal and plant life there, even though the change may be so small as to be unmeasurable. Biological monitoring for detectable changes has the attraction that aquatic organisms will be reacting to the totality of the inputs, both in terms of the variety of chemicals present and the range of their concentrations. In this respect, the measurement of biological responses has a distinct advantage over a chemical monitoring programme. Probably the most comprehensive review of the use of biological monitoring in environmental management is that by Hellawell (1986). A useful introduction is given by Abel (1989), and a succinct survey of the current situation and suggestions for the direction of future research in this field has been published by the British Ecological Society (1990).

Measurement of changes

There is a long history to the development of methods of measuring changes in the structure of aquatic communities, particularly in response to organic polllution. Some organisms are apparently sensitive to reductions in the DO of the water, whereas others are more tolerant; however, it may be more accurate to say that the changes recorded are associated with changes in the DO because it is possible that there are other factors in complex organic effluents which are responsible in part for the effects on the organisms. These effects can be analysed in two basic ways: the presence or absence of 'key' species that span the spectrum of sensitivity to organic pollution, and the change in species diversity which is a reflection of the smaller number of tolerant species that are able to live in polluted water.

Of these two approaches, the identification of key species is the less time-consuming and this is important for routine monitoring programmes. Several samples have to be taken at each monitoring station to allow for spatial differences in the distribution of the organisms; even where the stream has a uniform substrate, the composition of the benthic communities can be 'patchy'. Therefore, the time taken to sort out the material and identify the species present can be considerable. The common practice is to sample the benthic invertebrates on the bed of the watercourse because they reflect the conditions at that site, whereas the organisms present in the water may reflect the conditions present at some distance upstream. This does not apply, of course, to samples taken in lakes and ponds.

The measurement of species diversity combined with the presence or absence of key species is probably the most sensitive method of detecting changes in the benthic community, although the identification of all the organisms to species or family level takes considerable time and expertise. The effort required increases if the abundance of the various species has to be recorded for the particular monitoring procedure. But here the quest for sensitivity in the method of analysis encounters the same problem as that found at the other end of the levels of organization shown in Fig. 4.1: it becomes increasingly difficult to evaluate the biological significance of the changes recorded, and to separate the effects of natural phenomena from those caused by man-made inputs into the aquatic environment.

Considerable advances have been made in recent years in the categorization of the types of benthic communities that should occur in different conditions of water flow rates and substrate formation, so that the extent to which the community at a sampling site deviates from normal can be calculated. In the UK, a method called the River Invertebrate Prediction And Classification System (RIVPACS) has been developed and its validity is being investigated. This system predicts the type of aquatic community that would be expected to occur at sites with specific physical and chemical characteristics. However, it is recognized that the attribution of a recorded change in community structure to a specific cause, and especially to a specific substance, will be difficult at the present level of knowledge in this area.

Clearly, if the changes were associated with a substantial upstream discharge of a sewage effluent, then the cause would be obvious but the information obtained would only support the results of chemical analysis and would not necessarily provide new information. But in a river receiving sporadic inputs from unsuspected sources it may be difficult to identify the cause of the problem from the results of a benthic survey. Therefore the use of biological monitoring to plug the gaps in a chemical monitoring programme is not an easy solution to the problem. As with other types of ecotoxicological information described in previous chapters the data have to be evaluated by experts who are aware of the limitations of the methodology used.

Relationship between fish and benthic populations

Finally, the results of benthic monitoring cannot be extrapolated to predict effects on the fish community. Obviously, a river which is so polluted that it is almost devoid of invertebrate life is unlikely to contain a flourishing populations of fish; at the other end of the scale, a river containing a benthic community that would be expected to occur in that particular habitat is likely to support an appropriate community of fish. Between these two extremes the correlation is much less obvious. The loss of a few invertebrate species that are much more sensitive than fish to a particular man-made input is unlikely to be reflected in a change in the fish community except in the rare event that an important and irreplaceable component of their diet has been lost. A review of the relationship between the results of biological monitoring and the status of fish populations is given by Alabaster (1977); although somewhat dated, some of the conclusions and recommendations remain valid.

The only way to assess whether the fish community in a water body deviates from that normally expected is to investigate the status of the fish populations themselves. This is also not an easy task. It is beyond the scope of this book to examine all the problems involved in assessing the status of a fish community but in many ways there are similarities with those for benthic communities. The added problems include the selective nature of the various methods of capture; neither electric fishing nor netting are effective for very small species and the juvenile stages of larger fish. Some locations such as very weedy or very deep rivers are difficult to survey with existing techniques. Furthermore, all methods of capture place a stress on the fish and their chances of survival on return to the water may be reduced. The techniques are time-consuming and not suited for routine monitoring with frequent sampling times. Angler's catch returns can be useful in a qualitative sense, although here again the problem of selectivity of capture occurs. Nevertheless, the fish species sought by fishermen represent the recreational and commercial value of the resource and I will return to this aspect later.

INCLUSION OF FISH IN WATER CLASSIFICATION SCHEMES

During recent decades, there have been several schemes proposed whereby stretches of rivers can be given a classification based on a few parameters reflecting the extent to which the water is polluted or contaminated. These parameters can be chemical or biological, or a mixture of the two. In the early

1960s, a map was constructed showing the distribution of fishless rivers in England and Wales, and the causes of the pollution there. However, the exercise was not repeated and it was not until the late 1970s that a national scheme was drawn up for the classification of rivers by the then National Water Council. This classification relied on three basic parameters − BOD, DO and ammonia − to separate waters into four classes (1A & 1B, 2, 3 and 4), and to reflect the suitability of such waters for potable water supplies; the general outline is shown in Table 8.2.

This classification scheme was designed to give general guidance on the state of UK rivers and so some flexibility was included in the derivation of the classes. It was recognized that although many rivers were affected by organic discharges from sewage treatment works and intensive agriculture, some were affected by other sources of pollution. Therefore, the classification based on the three above-mentioned parameters, could be adjusted downwards if there was evidence that other substances were present that caused a deterioration in water quality.

Relevance to fish

The status of the fish populations was not an integral part of the classification. Rivers in Classes 1 and 2 were expected to support good salmonid and good coarse fisheries respectively, and the water quality of both classes was expected to be suitable for fish 'in EIFAC terms'. It is not clear whether this latter requirement referred to the EIFAC-proposed water quality standards or the general statement that these waters should enable fish to flourish throughout their whole life cycle. Nevertheless, it seems likely that the status of the fish populations was taken into account in reclassifying rivers which were on the borderlines of the four classes. To that extent, the compliance with EIFAC standards will approximate to that of the EC Freshwater Fish Directive.

Table 8.2 Simplification of the River Water Classification Scheme (England and Wales) (DOE 1986)

Parameter (95 percentile values)	Classes				
	Good		Fair	Poor	Bad
	1A	1B	2	3	4
Dissolved oxygen (DO) % saturation	>80	>60	>40	>10	<10
Biochemical oxygen demand (BOD) mg/l	<3	<5	<9	<17	>17
NH_3 mg N/l	<0.4	<0.9	>0.9		
EC Fish Directive (equivalent to EIFAC values)	Complies with salmonid standards		Complies with coarse fish standards		
1985 Survey % river length (total = 38 900 km 24 170 miles)	34	34	22	9	2

Value and limitations

This pragmatic approach is acceptable for producing a generalized summary of the state of the nation's rivers but because of the subjectivity involved it cannot be used within a legal framework of pollution control. This is because definitive proof would be required that a water quality class had been achieved in a stretch of water. Even the measurements of the three basic parameters are subject to variability, not only in the precision of the measurements themselves but also in the extent to which a few samples can adequately describe the quality of the river water, as shown in previous chapters.

For example, if a Class 1 river was on the borderline between Classes 1 and 2, a considerable deterioration in water quality would have to occur before the river was reclassified downwards; the measurement of a smaller deterioration might be the result of chance in that the samples taken just happened to coincide with the worst conditions, compared with a more faithful reflection of the average quality obtained in previous years. Conversely, a Class 2 river might have to show a considerable improvement over and above the minimum requirement for Class 1 before it could be reclassified upwards. The classification of a river, therefore, might depend on the initial class to which it was assigned — substantial changes would need to occur before its class was changed. A situation could arise in which a poor Class 1 river was in a worse state than a good Class 2 watercourse.

Despite these problems, classification schemes can be extremely valuable in informing the public of the present status of river water quality, particularly because this information can be displayed on maps so that the location and extent of the polluted areas are readily visible. Changes in the lengths of river that fall into the various classes provide an indication of the extent to which their quality is improving or deteriorating, bearing in mind that minor changes can be caused by climatic factors.

It would be unwise, however, to rely on such a classification to protect freshwater fisheries. The discretionary designation of waters under the EEC Directive for the protection of fresh-water fish does display an intention in this direction, even though the chemical parameters monitored may not be comprehensive and peak levels of contaminants may go unrecorded. There would seem to be a case for waters to be designated in terms of the uses to be made of them; such designations would be agreed by the local interested parties. Thus, it might be agreed that a stretch of river should support a good coarse fishery, with some of the important species identified. This approach has been adopted for some rivers in Eastern England and gives some encouragement for the future.

However, the same problems exist; how can the status and general wellbeing of the fish community be measured with any accuracy? If the fishery seems to be deteriorating, is it because of natural causes, bad fisheries management practices or pollution? The different possibilities provide scope for endless disagreements. Nevertheless, the science of fisheries management is continually improving and on balance the main plank in the protection of this resource may be the designation of the types of fishery which should be maintained and improved in different stretches of water. Clearly, all the other controls on water quality and the associated monitoring are important in providing evidence of changes in the types of inputs which may affect fisheries, but these should be seen as supportive of the main commitment to protect, maintain and improve fish populations.

CONCLUSIONS

It is clear that there is a wide range of measures that can be taken in order to protect the quality of surface waters. All have their individual values and limitations, and these must be recognized if they are to be effective. No single measure is of overriding importance; each makes a unique contribution to the prevention and control of pollution. Accordingly, it is necessary to strike the right balance in allocating resources for the execution of these measures, so that the maximum amount of useful information is obtained from the effort expended. This is especially important in the context of cost-benefit-analysis for environmental protection.

9 The Economic Value of Freshwater Fisheries

Previous chapters have provided an outline of the effects of harmful chemicals on fish and methods of pollution control and prevention. Remedial measures to reduce the input into water of chemicals from point and diffuse sources can be costly and although the expenditure can be distributed between several water uses, particularly the use of water for domestic consumption, a significant proportion of the cost must be associated with the protection of fisheries. As the general public demand for a cleaner environment gathers pace, so increasing care has to be taken to ensure that the scarce financial resources available are used to the best effect and produce a tangible benefit. Why, then, are freshwater fisheries so important as to warrant especial attention compared with that given to the other species of freshwater life?

AS A SOURCE OF FOOD

At a basic level, freshwater fish have been an important source of protein in the past for those countries that are now developed, and this remains so for those that are less developed. Fish farming is increasing in importance as a means of converting protein which is not normally eaten by man into an acceptable edible product, and water supplied to these farms has to be of a good quality. To some extent the development of fish farms is taking the pressure off the over-exploitation of valuable natural fish stocks; also, for those countries that have a ready access to marine stocks of fish and shellfish the importance of freshwater fish as a component of the diet is much reduced.

However, it must be recognized that in developed, densely populated countries which have the most pressing pollution problems the importance of natural freshwater fish stocks as part of the national diet is very small indeed, even for luxury species such as salmon and eels. The value of the commercial catch can be readily calculated, although it is likely to be an underestimate because the data do not include catches that have been made by methods that are not legal or not reported for other reasons.

SPORTING VALUE

Paradoxically, it is in these developed countries that the recreational value of fisheries has become of greater importance, associated with increased time for leisure activities. There can be no doubt that fishing is a very popular sport and it probably fills a deep-seated need by man to hunt a wily quarry with skill and patience; also, it has the advantage of presenting less of a danger or aggravation to other members of the public than other forms of hunting!

Although there have been several attempts to assess the value of fishing for sport in financial terms, none have been entirely satisfactory. The value of a stretch of water as a fishery can be readily assessed on its market sale value, or on the rent that can be charged. Less easy to assess is the amount that fisherman are prepared to pay for travel and equipment in the pursuit of their sport, or the value of the supporting infrastructure. And even then, consideration has to be given to the possibility that if there was no recreational fishing available, the money now spent on that sport would be allocated to some other activity (such as bowls?) without affecting the economy of the country.

COST OF FISHERIES PROTECTION

But should the fisherman then bear the total cost of fisheries protection? If the riparian owner has the common law expectation that his waters should contain fish, then it is clear that the polluter should pay the costs of achieving this objective, leaving the fisherman to bear the costs of fisheries management. But this still leaves open the question of where to allocate the costs of water quality monitoring.

Rivers can vary in quality between those that are in their natural state, virtually unaffected by human activity, and those that drain industrial conurbations and are almost devoid of higher forms of life. Not all rivers can be in the former state and so, as shown in Fig. 2.2, Chapter 2, there has to be a level of change that is deemed acceptable. The presence of a flourishing fish community in a river or lake can be taken as a yardstick of satisfactory water quality and satisfactory communities of associated freshwater organisms. Certainly, the public appreciate the value of fish as an indicator of water quality, as shown by the outcry when an accidental spillage causes a spectacular fish kill. To some extent this derives from a visual appreciation of the disaster; a mass mortality of midge larvae would go unnoticed or, even if visible, attract much less public concern.

NATIONAL COMMITMENT TO PROTECT FISHERIES

There must be a national commitment to protect the freshwater fisheries in rivers and lakes, not only because of their food and recreational value but as an indication of a satisfactory biological water quality. This should not be deflected by the growing importance of still-water fisheries which are becoming established in large ponds and lakes; these provide an enclosed area where fisheries management is easier and the water quality can be maintained more readily than in rivers where upstream discharges are beyond the control of an angling club. Initiatives in this direction may reduce the pressure to maintain riverine fisheries, but the national commitment to their preservation must remain and the cost of monitoring these waters should be borne by central funds.

DEVELOPMENT OF NEW ECONOMIC MODELS

Although this approach would seem to be entirely logical in principle, it will still be difficult to place a monetary value on freshwater fisheries as a resource, in other words to quantify the value of the benefits against which to compare the costs of their protection. The ability to make such an assessment is becoming essential in both developed and developing countries and this has led to the beginnings of a closer integration between environmental toxicologists and economists in order to devise the appropriate concepts and models. A review of the present situation is given in Opschoor and Pearce (1991) in which a number of environmental economic models are described, together with some of the associated ecotoxicological problems. Figure 9.1 shows how economic evaluations, environmental risk assessments and public (and political) pressure should be integrated to achieve the goal of fisheries protection. It is clear that there is scope for improvement in all these three factors, not least in ensuring that the public is better informed about the realities of pollution.

It is essential, in this context, that fisheries biologists and fishermen begin to quantify the concept of an acceptable fish community in order to provide a defensible yardstick against claims so often heard that the fishing is not as good as it was. The cause of any real decline should be properly identified and not just attributed to pollution as an easy explanation. This is where sound data on the status of existing fish populations are essential, despite the problems outlined in Chapter 8, together with a knowledge of the potential carrying capacity for fisheries in those waters.

It is possible that in some cases, such as small fishless streams in industrialized areas, the cost of effluent treatment and control may far exceed the value of any fishery that could be developed there and it may be necessary for the status quo to be accepted for the time being. The loss of such a potential fishery would be more than balanced if the same amount of money was spent in improving more marginal

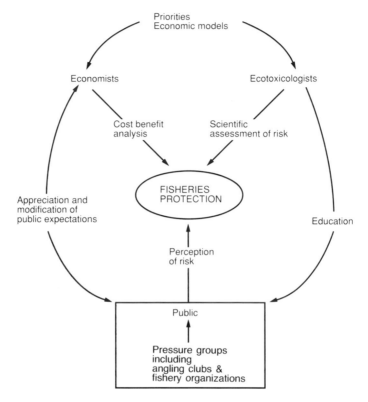

Fig. 9.1 Interrelationships between economists, ecotoxicologists and the public in the protection of fisheries (adapted from Lloyd 1991).

rivers where only relatively small improvements were needed to bring their quality up to the required standard.

The proper allocation of financial resources is undoubtedly an area which needs to be developed in order to maximize the effectiveness of environmental programmes in cost benefit terms. What is not in doubt, however, is the prime need to protect, maintain and improve the national freshwater fish communities, and there is every reason to hope that this will continue to be a well-defined national objective.

10 General Conclusions

The main objective of this book has been to describe how the aquatic environment is in a continuous state of change, with fluctuations following a daily and seasonal cycle on which climatic events of rainfall are superimposed. Man-made inputs can also fluctuate, from semi-continuous discharges to sporadic events. It is impossible to record all these changes with any accuracy by the use of chemical or biological monitoring. Similarly, the sensitivity of fish to toxic chemicals can vary with the natural changes in water quality. Accurate information exists on the effects of these chemicals on fish under laboratory conditions of continuous exposure to set concentrations, and little is known of the effects of the fluctuating exposures that are encountered in the field. Therefore, making a quantitative assessment of the actual input of a chemical into surface waters, of the dilution it will receive, of the likely fluctuations in the water quality characteristics and the effect which these will have on the sensitivity of the fish, is very difficult, if not impossible, for most substances.

It is these complexities and uncertainties, well-known to ecologists, that can become magnified by fear and thus lead to the conclusion that the only certain way to protect the quality of our lakes and rivers is to reduce all discharges and man-made inputs to a minimum and ideally to zero. But this is clearly not only an unrealistic goal but also economically wasteful in cost-benefit terms. Therefore, an attempt has to be made to identify and rank in order of importance those chemicals and effluents which are harmful to the environment and in particular, in the context of this book, to fish. Therefore, research should continue to be directed towards reducing the uncertainties that exist at present. Considerable progress has been made in recent years in quantifying the effects of mixtures of chemicals on fish. Associated with these studies has been a rapid development in the use of quantitative structure activity relationships that bring new insight into the types of toxic action of chemicals and the prediction of concentrations that have a harmful effect. Increasingly, confident predictions can be made of the concentrations of chemicals above which fish can be harmed. There is still some uncertainty in the prediction of acceptable concentrations for the protection of the whole spectrum of other aquatic species but the research programmes outlined above will go some way towards reducing these uncertainties.

Probably the major uncertainties are in the prediction and measurement of environmental concentrations of chemicals. But even here it is possible to make an estimate of the range of concentrations that are likely to occur; attention can then be given to those substances whose range overlaps the levels harmful to fish. With the increasing sensitivity of chemical analysis, many more substances will be found in water at extremely low concentrations. There will always be a temptation to equate the mere presence of such substances with potential harm, even though in practice the concentrations are so low as to be harmless either alone or in combination with similar quantities of other substances. What is required, therefore, is a method of expressing the risk of harm in numerical terms that indicate, for example, that the chance of a given concentration causing harm to fish is one in a million. This would help to put the risk of damage into perspective. Information of this type is necessary in another context — that of identifying the cause of a poor fishery in a river or lake. As shown in Chapter 1, there are several ways by which man's activity can affect fish populations, as well as natural factors. It would be wasteful of resources if chemical pollution was wrongfully identified as the cause of a poor fishery so that after expensive remedial action to remove inputs the problem still remained. Also, the delay in identifying the true cause may be critical in that it could prevent successful recovery of a balanced fish community.

Finally, there is the problem of monitoring the concentrations of chemicals in the aquatic environment in order to check that water quality standards are being met. Both chemical and biological methods have their limitations, but paradoxically their effectiveness will be increased as their shortcomings are fully recognized. There is no method of legislation and enforcement that can guarantee the safety of fish from pollution; there is always the problem of unidentified and unsuspected substances which can cause harm. But when properly used, the methods of control described in previous chapters can go a long way towards protecting fish from known causes of harm.

Perhaps the best guarantee of success will be a general public acceptance that a flourishing fish community is an important measure of an acceptable quality of water in our rivers and lakes. This will then put the onus on the fisheries managers to define the status of the fish populations which they would expect to find in their waters, so that deviations attributable to chemical pollution can be identified. But it must be re-emphasized that chemical pollution is only one way whereby man's activities can affect the wellbeing of fish. Continued vigilance and the further acquisition of knowledge on the totality of environmental effects will be required in order to protect the fish communities that form a most valuable and precious resource in our rivers and lakes.

References

Abel P.D. (1989) *Water pollution biology*. Ellis Horwood Ltd., Chichester.

Abel R., Hathaway R.A., King N.J., Vosser J.L. & Wilkinson T.G. (1987) Assessment and regulatory actions for TBT in the UK. *Oceans*, **4**, 1314–1319.

Alabaster J.S. (1977) *Biological Monitoring of Inland Fisheries*. Applied Science Publishers Ltd., London.

Alabaster J.S., Calamari D., Dethlefsen V., Konemann H., Lloyd R. & Solbe J.F. (1988) Water quality criteria for European freshwater fish: Effects of toxicant mixtures in water. *Chemistry and Ecology*, **3**, 165–253.

Alabaster J.S. & Lloyd R. (1982) *Water Quality Criteria for Freshwater Fish*, 2nd ed. Butterworth Scientific, London.

Bergman H.L., Kimerle R.A. & Maki A.W. (1986) *Environmental hazard assessment of effluents*. Pergamon Press, SETAC Special Publications Series, New York.

British Ecological Society (1990) *River water quality. Ecological Issues No. 1.*, Field Studies Council, Shrewsbury.

Crossland N.O. (1982) Aquatic toxicology of cypermethrin. II. Fate and biological effects in pond experiments. *Aquatic Toxicology*, **2**, 205–222.

DOE (1986) *River quality in England and Wales 1985*. HMSO, London.

Douben P.E.T. (1989) Metabolic rate and uptake and loss of cadmium from food by the fish *Noemacheilus barbatulus* L. (Stone loach). *Environ. Pollut.*, **59**, 177–202.

EEC (1976) Directive (76/464/EEC) on pollution caused by certain dangerous substances discharged into the aquatic environment of the Community. OJ L129, 18.5.76.

EEC (1978) Directive (78/659/EEC) on the quality of fresh waters needing protection or improvement in order to support fish life. OJ L222, 14.8.78.

EEC (1979) Directive (79/831/EEC) amending for the sixth time Directive 67/548/EEC on the approximation of the laws, regulations and administrative provisions relating to the classification, packaging and labelling of dangerous substances. OJ L259, 15.10.79.

EIFAC: Technical Reports on Water Quality Criteria for European Freshwater Fish, FAO, Rome, Italy. Technical Papers: TP1 Suspended solids (1964); TP4 Extreme pH values (1968); TP6 Temperature (1968); TP11 Ammonia (1970); TP15 Monohydric phenols (1972); TP19 Dissolved oxygen (1973);

TP20 Chlorine (1973); TP21 Zinc (1973); TP27 Copper (1976); TP30 Cadmium (1977); TP43 Chromium (1983); TP45 Nickel (1984); TP46 Nitrite (1984); TP37 Rev. 1 Mixtures of toxicants (1987).

GESAMP (1980) *Report of the eleventh Session. Reports and Studies No. 10.* UNEP. (GESAMP − IMO/FAO/UNESCO/WMO/WHO/IAEA/ UN/UNEP Joint Group of Experts on the Scientific Aspects of Marine Pollution.)

Haig A.J.N., Curran J.C., Redshaw C.J. & Kerr R. (1989) Use of mixing zone to derive a toxicity consent condition. *J. IWEM.*, **3**, 356−365.

Haigh N. (1987) *EEC environmental policy and Britain*, 2nd ed. Longman Group UK Ltd., Harlow.

Haux C. & Forlin L. (1988) Biochemical methods for detecting effects of contaminants on fish. *Ambio.*, **17**, 376−380.

Hoar W.S. & Randall D.J. (1984) *Fish physiology. Vol. 10. Gills.* Part A: Anatomy, gas transfer and acid-base regulation. Academic Press, New York.

Hellawell J.M. (1986) *Biological indicators of freshwater pollution and environmental management.* Elsevier, London.

Howells G., Dalziel T.R.K., Reader J.P. & Solbe J.F. (1990) EIFAC water quality criteria for European freshwater fish. Report on aluminium. *Chemistry and Ecology*, **4**, 117−173.

Kaiser K.L.E. (1984) *QSAR in environmental toxicology.* D. Reidel Publishing Co, Dordrecht.

Kaiser K.L.E. (1987) *QSAR in environmental toxicology − II.* D. Reidel Publishing Co, Dordrecht.

Lloyd R. (1961) The toxicity of mixtures of zinc and copper sulphates to rainbow trout (*Salmo gairdnerii* Richardson). *Ann. Appl. Biol.*, **49**, 535−538.

Lloyd R. (1986) Some common sources of error in data derived from toxicity tests on aquatic organisms. In *Toxic hazard assessment of chemicals* (Ed. by M. Richardson). The Royal Society of Chemistry, Burlington House, London.

Lloyd R. (1991) Some ecotoxicological problems associated with the regulation of PMPs. In *Persistent pollutants: Economics and Policy.* (Ed. by J.B. Opschoor & D.W. Pearce), pp 203−209. Kluwer Academic Publishers, Dordrecht.

MAFF (1989) *Report of the Working Party on Pesticide Residues, 1985−88.* Food Surveillance Paper No. 25. HMSO, London.

Matthiessen P., Whale G.F., Rycroft R.J. & Sheahan D.A. (1988) The joint action of pesticide tank-mixes to rainbow trout. *Aquatic Toxicology*, **13**, 61−76.

Opschoor J.B. & Pearce D.W. (1991) *Persistent pollutants: Economics and Policy.* Kluwer Academic Publishers, Dordrecht.

Park S.S. & Uchrin C.G. (1988) A numerical mixing zone model for water quality assessment in natural streams: Conceptual development. *Ecological Modelling*, **42**, 233−244.

Pentelow F.T.K. (1953) *River purification.* Edward Arnold and Co., London.

Rand G.M. & Petrocelli S.R. (1985) *Fundamentals of aquatic toxicology.* Hemisphere Publishing Corporation, Washington.

Randall D.J. & Wright P.A. (1987) Ammonia distribution and excretion in fish. *Fish Physiology and Biochemistry,* **3**, 107–120.

Richardson M. (1986) *Toxic hazard assessment of chemicals.* The Royal Society of Chemistry, Burlington House, London.

Royal Commission (1912) *Royal Commission on sewage and sewage disposal; Eighth report.* HMSO, London.

Saunders R.L. & Sprague J.B. (1967) Effects of copper-zinc mining pollution on a spawning migration of Atlantic salmon. *Wat. Res.,* **1**, 419–432.

Speare D.J. & Ferguson H.W. (1989) Fixation artifacts in rainbow trout (*Salmo gairdneri*) gills: A morphometric evaluation. *Can. J. Fish. Aquat. Sci.,* **46**, 780–785.

Sprague J.B. (1969) Measurement of pollutant toxicity to fish. I. Bioassay methods for acute toxicity. *Wat. Res.,* **3**, 793–821.

Sprague J.B. (1970) Measurement of pollutant toxicity to fish. II. Utilizing and applying bioassay results. *Wat. Res.,* **4**, 3–32.

Sprague J.B. (1971) Measurement of pollutant toxicity to fish. III. Sublethal effects and 'safe' concentrations. *Wat. Res.,* **5**, 245–266.

Sprague J.B. (1973) The ABC's of pollutant bioassay using fish. In *Biological methods for the assessment of water quality* (Ed. by J. Cairns Jnr & K.L. Dickson), pp. 6–30, ASTM STP 528. American Society for Testing and Materials, Philadelphia.

Stott B. & Cross D.G. (1973) The reactions of roach (*Rutilus rutilus*) to changes in the concentration of dissolved oxygen and free carbon dioxide in a laboratory channel. *Wat. Res.,* **7**, 793–805.

Turing H.D. (1952) *River pollution.* Edward Arnold and Co, London.

Vouk V.B., Butler G.C., Upton A.C., Parke D.V. & Asher S.C. (1987) *Methods for assessing the effects of mixtures of chemicals.* (SCOPE 30, IPCS Joint Symposium 6, SGOMSEC 3). John Wiley and Sons, Chichester.

Waite M.E., Evans K.E., Thain J.E. & Waldock M.J. (1989) Organotin Concentrations in the Rivers Bure and Yare, Norfolk Broads, England. *Applied Organometallic Chemistry,* **3**, 383–391.

Water Authorities Association (1986) *Mixing zones: Guidelines for definition and monitoring.* London.

Water Research Centre. Proposed environmental quality standards for List II substances in water. WRc Environment-ESSL, PO Box 16, Marlow, Bucks, UK. TR207 Chromium; TR208 Inorganic lead; TR209 Zinc; TR210 Copper; TR211 Nickel; TR212 Arsenic; TR253 Vanadium; TR254 Inorganic tin; TR255 Organotins; TR256 Boron; TR257 Sulphide; TR258 Iron; TR259 pH; TR260 Ammonia; TR261 Mothproofing agents.

Whale G., Sheahan D. & Matthiessen P. (1988) The toxicity of tecnazene, a potato sprouting inhibitor, to freshwater fauna. *Chemosphere,* **17**, 1205–1217.

Wright P.A., Heming T.A. & Randall D.J. (1986) Downstream pH changes in water flowing over the gills of rainbow trout. *J. Exp. Biol.,* **126**, 499–512.

Index